T0339028

TO CARL SCHMITT

INSURRECTIONS:
CRITICAL STUDIES
IN RELIGION, POLITICS,
AND CULTURE

INSURRECTIONS: CRITICAL STUDIES IN RELIGION, POLITICS, AND CULTURE

Slavoj Žižek, Clayton Crockett, Creston Davis, Jeffrey W. Robbins, editors

The intersection of religion, politics, and culture is one of the most discussed areas in theory today. It also has the deepest and most wide-ranging impact on the world. Insurrections: Critical Studies in Religion, Politics, and Culture will bring the tools of philosophy and critical theory to the political implications of the religious turn. The series will address a range of religious traditions and political viewpoints in the United States, Europe, and other parts of the world. Without advocating any specific religious or theological stance, the series aims nonetheless to be faithful to the radical emancipatory potential of religion.

After the Death of God,
    John D. Caputo and Gianni Vattimo, edited by Jeffrey W. Robbins
The Politics of Postsecular Religion: Mourning Secular Futures,
    Ananda Abeysekara
Nietzsche and Levinas: "After the Death of a Certain God,"
    edited by Jill Stauffer and Bettina Bergo
Strange Wonder: The Closure of Metaphysics and the Opening of Awe,
    Mary-Jane Rubenstein
Religion and the Specter of the West: Sikhism, India, Postcoloniality, and the Politics of Translation,
    Arvind Mandair
Plasticity at the Dusk of Writing: Dialectic, Destruction, Deconstruction,
    Catherine Malabou
Anatheism: Returning to God After God,
    Richard Kearney
Rage and Time: A Psychopolitical Investigation,
    Peter Sloterdijk
Radical Political Theology: Religion and Politics After Liberalism,
    Clayton Crockett
Radical Democracy and Political Theology,
    Jeffrey W. Robbins
Hegel and the Infinite: Religion, Politics, and Dialectic,
    edited by Slavoj Žižek, Clayton Crockett, and Creston Davis
What Does a Jew Want? Arguing an End to an Artificial Conflict,
    Udi Aloni

TO CARL SCHMITT

LETTERS AND
REFLECTIONS

JACOB TAUBES

TRANSLATED BY KEITH TRIBE

WITH AN INTRODUCTION BY
MIKE GRIMSHAW

Columbia University Press　*New York*

Columbia University Press
Publishers Since 1893
New York   Chichester, West Sussex
cup.columbia.edu
Ad Carl Schmitt. Gegenstrebige Fügung
copyright © 1987 Merve Verlag, Berlin
Copyright © 2013 Columbia University Press

Library of Congress Cataloging-in-Publication Data

Taubes, Jacob.
[Ad Carl Schmitt. English]
To Carl Schmitt: letters and reflections / Jacob Taubes;
translated by Keith Tribe.
p. cm. — (Insurrections)
Includes bibliographical references.
ISBN 978-0-231-15412-3 (cloth)
—ISBN 978-0-231-52034-8 (e-book)
1. Taubes, Jacob—Correspondence. 2. Schmitt, Carl, 1888–1985—Corre-
spondence. 3. Political scientists—Germany—Correspondence. I. Title.

JC263.T38A4 2013
320.53'3092—dc23   2012035759

Cover image: (original photograph) © Jan Bickerton / Trevillion Images
Cover design: Lisa Hamm

PUBLICATION OF THIS BOOK
IS SUPPORTED BY A GRANT FROM
**JEWISH FEDERATION
OF GREATER HARTFORD**

CONTENTS

INTRODUCTION: "A VERY RARE THING"   ix
    MIKE GRIMSHAW

CARL SCHMITT: APOCALYPTIC PROPHET
OF THE COUNTERREVOLUTION   1

LETTER TO ARMIN MOHLER   19

APPENDIX: FOUR PASSAGES FROM LETTERS
OF CARL SCHMITT TO ARMIN MOHLER   25

LETTER TO CARL SCHMITT   27

EXTRACT FROM A DISPUTE ABOUT CARL SCHMITT   33

1948–1978: THIRTY YEARS OF REFUSAL   49

EDITORIAL NOTE   59
    PETER GENTE

    NOTES   61

INTRODUCTION

"A VERY RARE THING"
MIKE GRIMSHAW

How can, how does one engage with *To Carl Schmitt*? For this slim collection of writings, comprising letters and lectures on Carl Schmitt by Jacob Taubes, is a fascinating volume that not only increases our knowledge of Taubes, it also demands a rethinking of the role of Schmitt in twentieth-century thought, in particular theology and philosophy. Most centrally, it forces—or I should say, in a Taubean-style polemic, should force—a reconsideration of what is meant, is undertaken, and eventuates when we use the term *political theology* to describe a particular intellectual and scholarly endeavor. For political theology of the twentieth century is so deeply intertwined with Schmitt that to undertake it is always, even if unknowingly or silently, to engage in, variously, a conversation, dialogue, debate, or argument with Schmitt. Jacob Taubes found himself in such an engagement from 1948 when he set out his questions and views in a letter that came to the attention of Schmitt. The letters and lectures in this volume chart, rechart, discuss, and attempt to explain at least part of this engagement.

A central recurring theme and self-questioning takes the form of an intellectual confession from Taubes, providing the background for how a Jewish scholar became a "friend" (Taubes's term) of a jurist of the Nazi state. Just how this came to be is discussed throughout the collection and compels a rethinking of the influence of German thought

on twentieth-century thought in the sense that to think philosophically in the twentieth century (and into the twenty-first) in the realms
of politics, theology—and where they meet in political theology—
is to think in the wake of Schmitt. As Taubes notes, even Walter Benjamin stated his debt to Schmitt.

The issues that arise out of this are complex and over the last three
decades involve the turn to Paul as political theorist by not only
Taubes but also those who have later done so, such as Badiou, Agamben, and Žižek, and the growing body of "political Paul" scholarship
that follows. For Paul, as the one who claims the overcoming of law
by grace, in effect could be argued to undertake the central sovereign
act of exception in Western culture. Not that Paul is sovereign, but
that Paul—or at least Paul's Christ—proclaims the new sovereignty of
grace over what becomes characterized (and, it can be stated, all too
often caricatured) as the old sovereign God of law. Schmitt's political theology in turn can be seen as what occurs when the Church's
pragmatic combination of grace and new law becomes secularized law,
that is, when the secularized State replaces the Church as authority
and now decides the exception without explicit reference to God. Yet
God is always there, even when absent, dead, or discounted, for God
is the silent reference of political theology, the supplanted sovereign
of human politics.

Schmitt's response to Taubes's first letter and Taubes's wrestling
with how and when finally to respond provide a central focus and in
turn raise issues for how we read Schmitt today. For this is a very "rich"
resource and thus, as well as contextualizing both Taubes and Schmitt
and their relationship, there are the wider issues of political theology,
twentieth-century political and theological history, and the letter as a
resource and text. As such this is also a glimpse into a lost world of conversation and thought that because of the Internet is gone. How many
of us save our e-mails for the future? Indeed the e-mail itself seems to
encourage a different style of communication, and this has an impact
upon what could be called the contemporary history of thought. Letters

addressed to an individual come to be collected and read by a wider audience and so change their reception and form. We read them for an insight into what can be called an unguarded moment whereby, in the privacy of words on the page, the writer directly "speaks" to a recipient, yet often with an eye and ear for a wider audience and reception. As such, letters allow the pretense of a privacy that is more often the conduit of public utterance, debate, comment, gossip, and description that sits closer to a conversation than a controlled and ordered paper or exposition. In letters the public-private divide is dissolved, for a letter is always potentially a public document, a public record, yet one controlled and disclosed by the intentions of its author.

Taubes was noted as "a master of smaller scholarly genres such as essays, interventions, reviews, letters and talks."[1] These letters and talks are confessional and digressive, whereby intellectual history, polemic, and questions combine into a distinctly Taubean genre that could also be termed gnostic, for, as other commentators have discerned, Taubes is at heart a thinker who transgresses borders between domains, playing them against each other or blending them.[2] The relationship with Schmitt, of Jew and German Nazi jurist, is therefore, from Taubes's perspective, given a gnostic transgression; the central issue of friend-enemy is here remade from the view and position of the one designated enemy. Yet, as will be come clear, what drew them together was antiliberalism, an antiliberalism searching for expression in the face of failed apocalypse, an antiliberalism that gains new urgency in a world where new forms of antihuman (that is antihistorical) apocalypse seem to be resurgent.

It is also important to remember that in this collection Taubes has a central claim that Schmitt is responsible for the recovery of ideology and that ideology in the twentieth century exists in reference—and debt (good and bad)—to Schmitt. In fact, Schmitt himself, in Taubes's reading becomes what I would term an intellectual sovereign in that he determines the exception that enables this relationship to occur. The Nazi jurist who, as Taubes declares, is by culture and Catholicism an anti-Semite decides in 1948 to make the exception for the Jew who as enemy is the only one who truly understands him. Ideology in the wake of Schmitt must therefore by nature also be complex and open to new relationships—even if firstly as an act toward self-understanding. In short, ideology demands the possibility of the sovereign exception, for, in a secular world, ideology is what premodern faith has become.

It is also important to start reading and engaging with this collection from a position that understands how Jacob Taubes described his relationship with Carl Schmitt: "We knew that we were opponents to the death, but we got along splendidly. We knew one thing: that we were speaking on the same plane. And that was a very rare thing."[3]

The writings contained in *To Carl Schmitt* were originally published in Germany in 1987. While translated versions of three of the writings ("Carl Schmitt: Thirty Years of Refusal," the letters to Armin Mohler [February 14, 1952] and to Carl Schmitt [September 19, 1979]) have previously appeared as appendixes to Taubes's *The Political Theology of Paul*, this new translation by Keith Tribe restores these writings into the larger collection that provides a fascinating, challenging, and important engagement with that "very rare thing," the relationship between a Jewish intellectual and philosopher of history and a one-time, and unrenounced, Nazi jurist who is the major political theorist of the twentieth century.

Taubes's statement sets the terms for engaging with this remarkable encounter, for, via Schmitt's friend-enemy distinction they were indeed "opponents to the death" and yet they also were speaking on the same plane, a plane of apocalypticism and counterrevolution.

A NOTE ON WHAT FOLLOWS: THE ANNOTATIVE HERMENEUTIC READER

The following introduction will take two intertwined forms. Firstly there is a discussion of the documents and the issues that arise from a close reading. Secondly the Taubes-Schmitt relationship is placed in the wider debate regarding Schmitt that has occurred over the past twenty-five years, especially since the turn to Schmitt by the left as signaled by the journal *Telos* in and after 1987. These two intertwined readings become expressed in what can be argued is an annotative reading arising from my heavily annotated copy of *To Carl Schmitt*. In a bastardized form of secular gentile midrash, my marginalia also exist as an annotative type of midrashic continuation, that is, the hermeneutics of the tradition of political theology into and out of the present context in which *To Carl Schmitt* is read. This introduction is also therefore a counternarrative taking its starting point from the challenge laid down in the postfoundational thought of Gianni Vattimo. For Vattimo, the death of God signals the birth of hermeneutics, for a postfoundationalist world enacts what he terms the age of interpretation. Arising in response to Nietzsche's aphorism "there are no facts, only interpretations, and of course this too is only an interpretation,"[4] the age of interpretation is qualified as an age of "not neutral but engaged knowledge because it is not placed at an ideal place that would claim to be external to the process."[5] That is, hermeneutics is the expression of knowledge that is necessarily provisional and contested, because the hermeneutic event is not an objective event that we respond to by thought, but rather a transformative event that changes our existence.[6] Reading this collection is a transformative hermeneutic event, for it is the response to what was such a transformative exchange between Taubes and Schmitt.

As such, this introduction is not comprehensive, but any introduction that sought to be would become a separate text in itself; rather it exists as the offerings of one reader, introducing possible ways to read this text and raising further questions to consider. Because Taubes repeats earlier narratives in later presentations, I have chosen to respond to them as I read them—as a reader's annotative hermeneutics—not to attempt to collate references into a series of defined and ordered subject discussions. For that would be to turn the texts into something other than how they were written—and presented—to be read and responded to. This introduction is therefore a short circuit insertion into what has become the public relationship and debate on the relationship of Taubes and Schmitt. Drawing on Benjamin, Agamben expresses the central importance of citation: "Just as through citation a secret meeting takes place between past generations and ours, so too between the writing of the past and present a similar kind of meeting transpires; citations function as go-betweens in this encounter."[7] Žižek's notion of the short circuit, its "secret meeting," occurs in this interchange. A major text and or author is "short-circuited" by reading via "a 'minor' author, text or conceptual apparatus. . . . If the minor reference is well chosen, such a procedure can lead to insights which completely shatter and undermine our common perceptions."[8] It is also important, in such a reading strategy, to remember that, for Benjamin, "to quote involves the interruption of its context."[9] Annotations are of course not quotations, but, in their interruption, they do offer a type of secret meeting and short circuit. What follows is therefore an annotative reading, a short-circuiting of *To Carl Schmitt*.

REREADING *TO CARL SCHMITT*

The collection begins with the transcript of a lecture on Schmitt, given by Taubes in Berlin in 1985 wherein Taubes attests to his respect for Schmitt, even though Taubes as a "conscious Jew" is one who is marked as "enemy" (1) by Schmitt.[10] This friend/enemy distinction sits at the center of their relationship and, as will be argued, also sits at the heart of how we, today, engage with Schmitt. In a further direction for our engagement, Taubes at the outset makes the interesting claim that to truly understand Schmitt one should not turn to his "major, clamorous texts" but rather should read his "broken confessions," which were published as *Ex Captivitate Salus* in 1950 and include the poem of the same name.

This poem, still only readily available in English via a translation in the journal *Telos*,[11] is perhaps the closest form we have to an autobiographical confessional statement. In it Schmitt describes himself as the one through whom "all the tribulations of fate" have passed; he is acquainted "with the abundant varieties of terror . . . and know[s] their grip" as well as "the chanting choirs of power and law."

Via this poem it is apparent Schmitt's self-positioning as the man through whom recent history has waged its confrontations with terror and chaos sits at the heart of his political theory. For chaos is Schmitt's great enemy, and the role of the sovereign is ultimately, in the face of chaos, to make the decisive judgment, the decision of the exception, the decision to keep order. In response to his own question "What now what shall I sing?" Schmitt sings anything but his rejected "the hymn of the placebo," and that is still his great attraction for thinkers on both the left and right; the question is, however, whether Schmittean medicine is really a cure.

What then is of value in being designated an "enemy" by Schmitt? Taubes argues that Schmitt's "enemy," defined from the perspective of a legal theorist, offers something that a theological definition does not. For the theological enemy is, according to Taubes (1), usually defined as one to be destroyed. The alternative possibility offered by the nontheological, legal enemy (that is, political theology) is that such an enemy must still be opposed, but not necessarily destroyed, because such an enemy is central to one's own self-identity. The caution arising is the reminder that to destroy the one who defines you is, in the end, to destroy oneself or, at the very least, to lose one one's self-identity. Yet the problem Taubes notes is that Schmitt's unrepentant move into an engagement with and within National Socialism does, however, put the legal theory definition of enemy in subservience to what I would define as the Reich theology definition of the enemy for National Socialism, wherein the enemy is to be destroyed. This question and its issues will continue to be engaged with by Taubes and Schmitt throughout this collection.

Yet, interestingly, such a question was not present for Taubes in 1942, when, aged nineteen and studying at the University of Zurich (his father was chief rabbi, having moved from Vienna in 1937), he came across reference to Schmitt's *Political Theology* in Karl Löwith's *From Hegel to Nietzsche*. What struck Taubes was Schmitt's allusion to the concluding verse of Baudelaire's *The Flowers of Evil* (1857) wherein Satan is elevated to the throne (and Taubes quotes [5]):

> Race of Cain, ascend to heaven
> And cast God down upon the earth!

Taubes took this opposition, via Löwith's tracing of an intellectual lineage "from Hegel via Marx and Kierkegaard to Nietzsche" (2) as the basis for a new historiography. The rejection of Taubes's argument by his professor was a turning point, for he found himself aligned with Schmitt's referencing of Hobbes's statement in *Leviathan* that "the law is made by authority, not by truth." In short, it was his encounter with Schmitt that made Taubes the type of thinker—and opponent to the professorial university and manner—he became for the rest of his life. What Taubes became instead was a philosopher of intellectual history, a philosopher grounded in history who remained opposed to the actions and thinking of most professional historians—especially those who aligned themselves to liberal modernity. This opposition to liberal modernity, and to liberalism more generally, is what holds the friend-enemy relationship of Taubes and Schmitt: a relationship conducted via a shared engagement with political theology, which Taubes reads from a politicotheological perspective, whereas Schmitt writes first and foremost as a jurist. It is this gap, this difference, of readings and perspectives that makes the Taubes-Schmitt debate so fascinating as well as important. For how, in the wake of both Taubes and Schmitt, do we today engage not only with Schmitt's *Political Theology* but also, more widely, the return and rise, indeed the expansion, of political theology as a claim, a vision, a hermeneutic, and a critique? Where does law (*nomos*) sit within political theologies? is the question Taubes was to memorably trace back to what he named as the political theology of Paul, especially the Letter to the Romans. Further, if, as Taubes states, the drive of political theology is that of "an apocalypse of the counterrevolution" (11), how is political theology as a movement to be rethought, for within such a redefinition apocalypse becomes a type of judgment central to any political theology and so makes political theology far more weighted toward theology than the political. It is here we are reminded of what has almost become the Schmittean cliché from *Political Theology* (1922) that "all significant concepts of the modern theory of the state are secularized theological concepts."[12] What if central to such a secularized move is the desire to keep the apocalypse at bay, to keep apocalyptic thinking at bay? Would—to push this further—the insight that theology, especially Christian theology, is inherently apocalyptic be the insight that liberalism in theology has striven so hard to cover up? Therefore is the exception, identified by Schmitt as analogous to the miracle,[13] the sign in the secular society of liberal modernity of the apocalyptic power that exists, that is referenced by both exception and miracle, that reminds us that what we believe to be the case, the norm, is in fact only fragile and transitory? Political theology therefore, as both the Schmitt book, but more as developing twentieth-century concept and critique, exists as a reminder of the apocalyptic in what is taken to be a secular world of the triumph of liberal democracy. Is, in fact, apocalyptic counterrevolution the real outside to liberal democracy, and is it this threat, this possibility of such chaos that lead, as Taubes comments, to the possibility that, as immediately post-Shoah as 1949, the Israeli minister of justice Pinchas Rosen was using the only available copy in Jerusalem of Schmitt's *Verfassungslehre* (*Constitutional Theory*, 1928) to attempt to draft a constitution for the state of Israel? (10–11). Was the model for Israel to be Weimar, a new Weimar in which article 48, that of presidential decree to protect public order, was imagined as a possibility to protect the newly emergent Jewish state against such chaos as led to the demise of Weimar? In effect, was the "enemy" Schmitt being used to draft a constitution to ensure the tragic exception would not be repeated? To answer such a question is beyond the scope of this introduction, but it is such questions that reading *To Carl Schmitt* raises.

It was this possibility, linked with the wider question of, as Taubes puts it "the problem of the Fascist intelligentsia" (11), specifically Schmitt and Heidegger[14] and of their Catholic background, that for Taubes could not be resolved "by appealing to the inner bastard of Nazism" (11). As can be seen in the "Letter to Armand Mohler," Taubes wrote of these issues to his one-time school friend and now extreme right-wing thinker and secretary to Ernst Jünger, who in turn passed it on to Carl Schmitt. At this same time Taubes was working toward what he terms "the apocalypse of the revolution," yet "free of the illusions of messianic Marxists" (11), in short, "a new concept of time and a new experience of history opened up by Christianity as an eschatology" (12). For Schmitt, the meeting point with Taubes comes via the notion of the katechon, the restrainer of the Antichrist, and the apocalyptic thought that follows. Yet, if they meet in apocalyptic thought, they come to this meeting place from different directions: Taubes from the bottom up, Schmitt from above, "from the powers that be" (13). What links them is "the experience of time and history as a delimited respite, as a term or even a last respite. Originally that was also a Christian experience of history" (13), and the katechon, as restrainer, is, as Taubes notes, part of how Christianity accommodated itself with the world when the expected End of the World failed to materialize. What is important to note is that Occidental history becomes what Taubes terms "that one-way street" (13) because of that expectation of the end of history. To assign such meaning to history, and to Occidental history within a framework of katechon, also influences how Occidental history is viewed—and experienced. A fascinating sidebar is that not only did Taubes present these ideas to a group at Harvard headed by a young Henry Kissinger, while in America he also taught Torah to a group of future neoconservatives including William Kristol and Gertrude Himmelfarb.[15] Taubes therefore also played his—unwitting—part in an early exposure of what were to become American neoconservatives to Schmittean-aligned thought, raising the fascinating question as to what degree could neoconservatism also be reread as a form of Schmittean katechon—especially with the influence of Leo Strauss? (It is beyond the scope of this introduction to follow such a line of thought, though it is important to note such possibilities—even for other scholars to contest them).

The relationship of Taubes and Schmitt was the result of Schmitt's letter to Armin Mohler, which was circulated initially throughout West Germany—and then wider afield—and occasioned Schmitt sending offprints and signed books to Taubes, who, while never refusing them, and reading every line, also never replied. This carries echoes of what Derrida discussed in his work on the gift,[16] which also puts the Taubes-Schmitt relationship in a new light, for this relationship that was to develop did not, on one level, include the indebtedness nor expectation that such "gifting" tends to involve. It is, while not being anonymous, actually far closer to a type of altruistic gifting that Derrida sees as true gifting. Yet conversely, the reason that Taubes did not respond to the ongoing gifting by Schmitt was Schmitt's "active anti-Semitism" (14), which is, as I will repeatedly remind readers, *the* issue that overshadows this whole relationship and the material in this collection—*as well*, of course, the use of Schmitt, especially by those on the left from the mid 1980s. This issue will continue to be raised and discussed as this introduction engages with the material, because each mention of it by Taubes raises slightly different questions.

What brought Taubes to reconsidering Schmitt was the challenge, in Berlin in 1967, of learning that the Russian-French Hegelian philosopher Alexander Kojève was going to Plettenberg to talk to Schmitt, identifying him as the only person in Germany worth talking to. Taubes, in considering this, tiess the common threads of apocalypticism in all three thinkers—himself, Schmitt, and Kojève—yet he, as one of the "chosen people," symbolized the subject of envy of those who considered themselves to be members of apocalyptic nations, that is, those who viewed themselves as the supersessionist nation, wherein nationalism exists as a version of replacement theology. It took years for Taubes to finally meet Schmitt in person, in Plettenberg, whereupon he and Schmitt had the "most violent" (15) discussion Taubes had ever undertaken in German, a discussion about historiography and myth. In referring to this discussion, Taubes focuses on the conflict between mythic images and terminology and positivism and historicism, a conflict in which Schmitt and Benjamin found themselves on the same side.

What does this mean for us today? Perhaps, if, as the American cultural critic Greil Marcus has noted (via Leslie Feidler), in the world of popular culture we are all imaginary Americans,[17] then in the world of political theology we are all imaginary Germans, or at least Weimar Germans. This claim is deliberately provocative, yet it might provide a way to understanding how and why the radical left—raised, as it were, on Benjamin—also came to see Schmitt as a friend-enemy ally from the mid 1980s onward.[18] If in political theology we find ourselves still in a mind-frame constructed by the debates of Weimar Germany, then our sources and solutions are going to be those who engaged in debate, discussion, and dialogue at that time. In effect, Schmitt creates the basis for modern political theology and so, dialectically, even to oppose him is to create a synthesis in which Schmitt is present, albeit transformed. Taubes notes this is what Benjamin did, inverting the "state of exception" from a dictatorial conception, "dictated from above" into "a doctrine in the tradition of the oppressed" (17). The result for both, according to Taubes, involves "a mystic conception of history whose principal teaching relates the sacred order to the profane" (17). This profane is not something that can be constructed upon a theocracy; thus, for both Schmitt and Benjamin, in Taubes's view, theocracy has "solely a religious significance" (17). According to Taubes's reading of Benjamin, secularization is the public face of rthe

Pauline-derived inner freedom of God's children, that is, secularization is the true outward expression of Christianity. Yet here Taubes suddenly concludes with a long quote from a 1924 review of *Political Theology* by the poet and Dadaist Hugo Ball in which the central claim is that Schmitt is responsible for the recovery of the respectability of ideology. Reading this via Taubes, the conclusion seems to be that ideology in the twentieth century followed (in all its variety of engagements) in the wake of Schmitt. Today, reading Taubes and Schmitt, at the conclusion of this first document, a question arises that takes us on from that earlier one of political theology being a form of imaginary Weimar Germany. If we remember the challenge of Benedetto Croce's maxim "We cannot not call ourselves Christians,"[19] perhaps we who engage in ideology, political theology, and associated philosophical undertakings find ourselves, at some point, confronted with the our own version of Croce's maxim whereby "We cannot not call ourselves Schmittean"?

We need to hold the tension of these questions as we turn to read that fateful letter, the letter that drives this whole collection, the one that instigates the relationship between Taubes and Schmitt, the "Letter to Armin Mohler" (14 February 1952).

This letter acts as type of theological hand grenade, forcing a reconsideration of what is involved in and with political theology, a debate that still rages today: for how do we and can we engage with one who aligns himself with/in National Socialism? This is, as Taubes notes at the time, a question also for Heidgger. There is a possible reading— that I acknowledge for many will be seen as a misreading—that here Taubes points toward assigning Schmitt to a type of sovereign— wherein the exception becomes problematic. The exception decision is that of deciding to align with National Socialism, for in a world where "humanism has run dry" (21) the question arises of who is sovereign now and what are the new states of exception, especially in the wake of the horrific consequences of the National Socialist state of exception. What is the new *nomos*—and can this only really be decided by those who posses "an inner connection to Germany" (21) to attempt to "explain, if at all possible, what happened and why?" (21).

Yet to complicate the issue is Taubes's observation that we have to ask theological questions in a context of a given fate of atheism; that is, how are we to ask theological questions of law in a world with the death of god and modern nihilism? For "we very much have to *live* in a post-Christian manner" (22), yet, as Taubes emphasizes by his italicization of *live,* the question is not that of merely existing, but the more direct and demanding one of living. Such questions were common in the postwar world; the horrific possibilities unleashed by the Shoah and the use of the A-bomb were coupled with the realities of the end of Christendom and the rise of the cold war, all of which raised a series of ontological and metaphysical questions that, it can be argued, were only exacerbated by the fall of the Berlin Wall in 1989 and the supposed triumph of what has become a neoliberal society. No wonder— it could be argued—the radical left reengaged with Schmitt, as in the infamous *Telos* debates of 1987, for what other tools were there that provided such a coherent if challenging alternative now that Marxism was believed by many to have failed?

Taubes, writing in 1952, sees political theology—and therefore Schmitt—as the way to engage with questions of law and *living* in a post-Christian manner, and because Christianity seems to have "turned down the problem" (22) of political theology, Judaism is now where political theology exists. Yet also, in a move that signals his political theology of Paul some thirty-five years later, Taubes notes how the exceptions to the law are "love, pity, (and real) forgiveness" (23), which, against his will, lead him back to St. Paul. Therefore the turn to Paul, as the root theologian of political theology, that has become so dominant in the past two decades, is that first signaled by Taubes in 1952, because it is Paul, in a moment that seeks to be post what was and is, who identifies those relations that exceed the law.

Taubes's letter is followed by short passages from letters from Schmitt to Mohler. The first sets the frame for what eventuates:

Taubes's interaction with Schmitt is not only "astonishing" (25), it is also found to be very moving by those Schmitt shows it to. This is in itself revealing, for remember this is only seven years after the end of the war. The important element is the final fragment, where Taubes's insight that today everything is theology except what is taken to be theology is recognized as his central brilliance (26). This in turn raises issues about what is theology in our contemporary world: is theology actually political theology and its associated relocations and associations into Continental philosophy? Is this in fact the triumph of theology in a secular society, and is this why, in particular, sociology appears to have lost its way? Recall that sociology was meant to replace theology; this was the drive from Comte through Weber and Durkheim; further, recall that the young Taubes traced the first appearance of Schmitt's political theology in volumes dedicated to Weber (4). And, yet, is not Habermas's turn to religion actually more a turn to theology than to religion itself, and did not Derrida declare to the American "death of God" theologian Altizer that he would pay to be a professor of theology (moreover, Julia Kristeva asked Altizer to think of her as the French death of God theologian)?[20] These digressions are in fact central to what sits at the heart of the Taubes-Schmitt relationship and why it continues to have such resonance: what if theology is what still drives us when we think most deeply philosophically and politically, when we think most deeply intellectually? Whether Jew or Gentile, atheist or believer, left or right, theology—and, it increasingly seems, the theology of Paul—shapes and drives our thinking, our wrestling, our questioning, our politics, our philosophy, our cultures, our very identities, yet, as Taubes notes—and Schmitt agreed—in a world in which we *have* to live in a post-Christian manner.

It is useful to digress to two American thinkers who offer a way to engage with these issues. Carl Raschke, tracing a lineage back to Kant, argues, "To think intensely what remains concealed in the depths of thought is to think theologically," and yet, because of the Enlightenment, such theological thinking has become "a very difficult, if not impossible, peculiar labor."[21] But today theology is also in a dialectic with deconstruction, whereby in post/modernity theology is now "a thought that has learned to think what is unthought within the thought of itself."[22] Or, as I would state, in post/modernity theology, if not sectarian, is the self-reflexivity of modern thought that thinks the unthought of both secularity and "religion." Philosopher of religion Charles Winquist notes the self-reflexivity of theology—that is, thinking about thinking—demands that then "we have to decide why we are calling any particular datum religious."[23] To this I would add the futher decisions regarding the designations *sacred, profane,* and *secular* as they have come to be used both in political theology and wider modernity. For secular, in particular, needs to be separated from secularist; that is, secular, as in "this-wordly" or, in the phrase of Gabriel Vahanian, "a world of shared human experience,"[24] is different from a position of being actively opposed to religion. Politcal theology operates, or has come to operate, as also a form of secular theology, and this is what is meant by Schmitt's statement (via Taubes): "today everything is theology, with the exception of what the theologians talk about" (26). Half a century on, it is still only the secular theologians and those influenced by Continental thought who have come to recognize that "everything is theology" and this is what puts them in opposition to theologians who still, paradoxically, talk about everything that is not theology. Or, as Taubes notes in his 1979 "Letter to Carl Schmitt," Erik Peterson identifies "the theological impossibility of a political theology" (28), which, in my reading could be countered by a view that political theology is theology versus theology, as theology in and of the katechon. Of course, this does not, as yet, take us any further.

So what is it that we need to talk about, if we wish to locate ourselves, our readings, our writing, our arguing within the theology that is not theologians' theology? Perhaps it is to deal with those central issues raised by Taubes and Schmitt, issues that are still yet to be resolved—if they indeed could be.

An issue to be resolved is that of "friend"; this arises from Schmitt's redefinition of politics along the divide of friend-enemy, and yet here, in Taubes's "Letter to Carl Schmitt," we have Taubes calling, in fact defining, Schmitt as "friend." This makes us redefine what is and can be meant by such a term, for we have the one who was, in Schmittean logic, the enemy of the Nazi state calling the one who defined Jews as the enemy "friend." Yet, as Taubes wryly, tragically observes, Jews were spared one thing in the horror that unfolded: they did not have to make a choice as to where they stood vis-à-vis Hitler and the Nazis, for Hitler made Jews "into absolute enemies" (27), and this disaster, a disaster for Jews and for everyone else, especially—so it seems to Taubes—for Germans, raises issues of how can we understand "the eschatological aspect of the disaster" (27). The critiques of Schmitt by Erik Peterson are discussed by Taubes in his letter, along with a reference to the psalmist's "true are the wounds that the arrow of a friend inflicts" (28); in fact, this appears to be a reference to Proverbs 27:6: "Better are the *wounds* of a *friend*, than the deceitful kisses of an enemy." If Peterson's critiques of Schmitt are those of the Christian "friend," is Taubes establishing himself as the Jewish "friend" inflicting wounds of truth? It would appear to be so, and this wounding by and of a friend is what sits at the heart of this correspondence, a wounding in the name and pursuit of truth.

Central to Taubes's questioning is how, in spite of the injunction of Romans 13 on obedience to the ruling state, the German Church was able to support a political "theozoology" (29), that is, a theology of classification in line with Nazi race theory. This is a question that has to go back before one of support for the ruling authorities to a question of creating and implementing a political theozoology that not only aligns with obedience to the ruling authorities but also underwrites, theologically, the creation of enemies and justifies attacks upon them. For Taubes, reading out of Hobbes's *Leviathan*, identifies the state as a mortal god that exists under the immortal God; therefore Jesus the Christ is that which/who can always overturn the mortal state in that the state, attempting to be immortal, sets itself against the immortal God. The task of political theology is thus to constantly redraw the boundary between the spiritual and the worldly, between what was the ecclesiastic and the civil power. Political theology is to ensure that there is a distinction between them, and to ensure that the civil power (the mortal power) does not usurp or attempt to overcome the distinction between it and what is today—in a post-Christian world—spiritual power, which is in reference to the immortal. In this discussion are the echoes of the claim by Taubes that he "had quickly come to see Carl Schmitt as an incarnation of Dostoevsky's Grand Inquisitor" (7): as one who defends the subversion of the Church to the interests of the State—even against the basis of the faith itself. For those then who follow in the wake of political theology, what may arise of Taubes's critique—if correct—that political theology is too often the theology of the Grand Inquisitor, whether that of Dostoevsky or, more recently, the Grand Inquisitor of Plettenberg? For if political theology, especially under Schmitt's direction, took on the role of the Grand Inquisitor, perhaps it was and is only the friend who is enemy—that is, those likewise involved in political theology who yet critique the Schmittean inversion of civil and ecclesiastic power—who can most truly wound, and wound in the name of truth. For central to political theology is the act of marking out the differences within political theology. And this act of marking out the difference is also central to Taubes's engagement with Schmitt.

Speaking in 1986, Taubes makes it very clear that, firstly, he is no German, but neither is he an apologist for Schmitt (33–34), rather his "very difficult problem" (34) is that he is a Jew, and this raises a central issues of how to judge. For, in having no choice, how can he judge? In short, Jews did not have to make the decision whether to and how to participate. For judgment can only arise, it appears in a Taubean conception, if you in some way can understand the possibilities, choices, and motivations of the other, of those who you are called upon to judge. What is left is a "problem of fascination" (34), a problem that for Taubes is exemplified with the decisions of both Schmitt and Heidegger to, in short, choose the Nazi alternative. For there seems to be, for Taubes, no way of understanding this from the perspectives of either contemporary history or the historical sciences (34). Further, in having made such a liaison, how could Schmitt and Heidegger meaningfully apologize, and indeed, how could all of those who made a similar choice of what Taubes defines, perhaps most tellingly, as "a phenomenon of *violence*"? (35). So Taubes's ongoing fascination with Schmitt is driven by his desire to understand National Socialism, and this also points to why Schmitt was so open to Taubes's questioning. For here was the enemy who asked the question expected to come from the friend: how could you have made such a choice? How do you explain your choice? In fact *can* you explain such a choices? And these are different questions from one of judgement, a question of judgement that as Taubes identifies, also involves those who were able to make such a choice now engaging in acts of forgetting, suppressing and displacement (35). The challenge is that of understanding "what kind of glittering dross this was" (35), a question all the more pertinent today with the return of extreme right-wing, nationalist movements across Europe. How could and why do such able minds succumb to the lure of glittering dross? Perhaps this is a question that can only be *engaged with* if asked in the nonjudgemental approach of the one made enemy without choice, for the betrayal here is so complete.

Therefore, in reading this correspondence, it becomes evident that Taubes's engagement with Schmitt is in both the realm and form of political theology, which became, of course, a modern nomenclature claimed by Schmitt for what he undertakes. Further, Schmitt, while being antiliberal, was not antidemocrat, but was in favor of a democratic dictatorship over and against liberalism. Therefore Taubes, in growing to understand Schmitt, also comes to understand the seeming oxymoron of democratic dictatorship and especially what can be said to be its lure for antiliberals of both left and right in the twentieth century. And in our understandings of Taubes and Schmitt we can also come to understand how the left, post–cold war, have come to engage with Schmitt as one offering what seems a way forward against liberalism and, more pertinently, against neoliberalism. As Taubes raises, there is an important question here in that what does the left's fascination with Schmitt tell us about the left? (36). How can the left turn to an extreme right theoretician and jurist to attempt to articulate a way forward? Yet this is nothing new, for the Frankfurt School, as Taubes comments (36), had been influenced by Schmitt in Weimar days; and such an influence continues, for Schmittean topics cross over into concerns also of the left for both left and right are concerned with what seems to them to be the failures and failings of liberalism.

It is here that friend-enemy becomes identified as the central concept, the concept that allows, if at first seemingly paradoxically, for the left to use the right-wing Schmitt or for the Jewish Taubes to be Schmitt's friend-enemy. The issue is firstly one of the justification of the distinction, a justification that is a justification from power, that is, it is a classification inherently linked to the power of the one who makes the classification. Taubes quotes from Schmitt's *The Concept of the Political* a most telling description in which it is the intensity of the relationship, a relationship determined by "union or separation" that is expressed as "association or disassociation" (37); the political enemy is first and foremost one who exists on the level of theory and practicality, that is, one who is "the other, the stranger" (37) and in that allows and in fact demands a identity from the one who classifies. In the Schmittean world, the only two identities that count are those of friend or enemy, everyone else is not worthy of notice or engagement; in fact they could be viewed as impediments to the real business of the friend-enemy engagement. They are impediments because they do not take seriously the questions that friend-enemy raise for both engaged in this relationship. In short, you have friends and you have enemies, and your enemy is also one who in an inverted sense is your friend because they 'get' what you get—but from the opposing perspective: they are engaged in a similar struggle, in similar questions, in similar dilemmas, if, from necessity, a point of opposition. As Taubes explains, Schmitt, in a private note written in a copy of *Ex Captivitate Salus*, made a claim that "affects us all: 'The enemy is our question given form', that is, one can see oneself in it" (37). In the discussion leading up to this statement, Taubes uses the example of how to classify war and the dangers arising if we decide to rebrand the one we oppose in war as a criminal instead of as an enemy. For if we do not allow war to exist as something we do as humans, something that we engage in, but an engagement that brings about peace, then war and engaging in it, and, most importantly, those who oppose us, who "provoke us" into a state of war, are criminal/criminals, and as criminals to be eliminated. So the liberalism that seeks to criminalize war, in fact, by criminalizing, seeks to eliminate those against whom one is forced into war; what this does is to overturn the traditional friend-enemy relationship, and instead one's identity is defined by an opposition to the criminal, who must be eliminated in order for *us* not to be defined *by* the criminal. Therefore, the question raised by Schmitt's note is whether it is better to have enemies as questions or enemies as criminals (37). And this is a relationship, a question that exists as the inverse, that is, Schmitt is the enemy as question *for* Taubes. Therefore friend-enemy are poised in a mutual interquestioning, an existential question to each other, a relationship in which, in effect, all others are excluded as those who are unable and incapable of asking, let alone answering the question/s. This is what the left and right, joining in Schmitt's friend-enemy against liberalism, do, for what they both get (that is, what they mutually understand)—from differing perspectives—is the problem of liberalism.

Yet for Taubes—and for *all* who read Schmitt in particular post-1945—there remains the central question of anti-Semitism. Schmitt is a Catholic thinker, and the position of the Catholic Church toward the Jews throughout most its history makes for a shameful record in the main. Protestants and Orthodox are likewise not excluded from this shame, this horror, and this is because of a Christian self-conception as to where it saw—and in the majority of believers, still sees—Christianity in relation to Judaism and Christians in relation to Jews. The question, baldly put, is whether Christianity the end, that is the supplanter, the supersessionism, of Judaism and therefore the rejection of Judaism's continuation. The Church that looks to a Jew as its savior is also the body that for much of its history persecutes, rejects, denies the validity of Judaism—and Jews as individuals. The culture of Christianity is a culture that ended in the death camps, in the Shoah. This is the central struggle that all Christians, in fact, that all who live in the wake of Christian culture must still wrestle with, must undertake and consider. Asked whether Schmitt—as a Catholic, as a theorist of Christian culture, of culture that arises out of a Christian society—is anti-Semitic or not, Taubes replies, "the Church is anti-Judaic, anti-Semitic" (38). The point is clear, the Church must first and foremost reconsider its identity, for the identity of the Church determines the identity of the culture and the individuals within it; even, as Taubes notes, in a society with a declining belief, the underpinnings of theology and the Church can too easily be manipulated to express a "theozoology" that replaces theology.

Whereas, in the context of Schmitt, Taubes sees this as a widespread Catholic issue, we today must not fall into a simplistic trap of seeing this as a particular, or even a majority, Catholic issue. Anti-Semitism is a Christian issue, a Christian culture issue, and an issue of the post-Christian and secular society that has arisen out of the collapse of Christendom; for while Christendom may have collapsed, anti-Semitism has not, and the roots of this are grounded in the attitudes, beliefs, and teachings of the Church over millennia. However, as can be also gathered from the reading of these letters, it is this that sits at the heart of the friend-enemy because, for Christians and Christianity, Jews and Judaism can, in the Schmittean sense, be seen as "the enemy is our question given," for "what does it mean to be Christian?" cannot be answered except with central reference to Judaism—then and now. That Schmitt and Taubes are friends-enemies is also part of their friend-enemy approach to the apocalyptic. The question of apocalypse from above is given form in apocalypse from below and vice versa. In all such questions is that central one of ontology: the one I see most clearly *as not me* demands a question to myself of *what am I to be*? This also is the reason the left turns to the right in the wake of the collapse of communism in 1989: what enables the right to survive when the left did not? Why did liberalism destroy the left and not the right? What can Schmitt—as central theorist of the right—tell the left as it seeks to redefine, relocate, resituate itself? For, as Taubes comments in his discussion on liberalism, liberalism comes at the cost of others; even if one would want to be liberal, "the world is not so made that one can be liberal" (38): if we are liberals who pays the cost—if liberalism triumphs, who pays the cost? For, in a line developed from Taubes, liberalism involves, in the end, a denial of the cost others suffer by our being liberal. That is, liberalism is not a neutral state of being, nor a neutral society, but a claim that is inherently oppositional and judgmental, with associated decisions and implementations, and such decisions are primarily focused on the benefits to the victors in what is seen as the inevitable march of human progress. Taubes's point is that liberal democracy fails to see what happens in history, which is a history of brutality. In short, liberals have too high a view of humanity and human nature, views that a realistic encounter with and examination of human history would quickly overturn.

Taubes is fascinated by Schmitt because in 1929 Schmitt stated that Central Europe lived in a crisis of legitimation, in effect between revolution and counterrevolution, existing under the eye of the Russians for over a century; Russians who, Schmitt claimed, would control the destiny of the century. And nothing had changed for either Taubes or Schmitt post–World War II compared to the world after World War I. In short, how does one restore a society where the choice seems to be a default one for a "depoliticized conventionality" (39), or a "depoliticized normality," a "cultural 'neutrality'" (39) that both Taubes and

Schmitt, as counterrevolutionaries, view as the expression of liberalism? Thus, for Taubes, Schmitt is compared to a prophet of crisis, counterrevolution, and antiliberalism, someone important for what he enables—and, in fact, demands—us to understand regarding Western history. And part of this is also what Taubes then identifies: that the state of exception is a fiction that happens just once in a lifetime (40). And therefore, following Taubes's provocation, the possibility emerges that Schmitt has been all too often misread, for the issue is not that of the sovereign deciding the exception but rather what does decision mean, and here reference is made back to Kierkegaard and the centrality of dialectical theology for the state of exception. Out of this discussion arises what can possibly be identified as the central tension of political theology, that is of both the Schmitt text and disciplinary definition, but also, for us today, of the political theology that has enjoyed both an intellectual and political resurgence: what does *pure* mean and thus, dialectically, what does *impure* mean? These are central to political theology, for *impure* is that which arises out of experience, language, and history; therefore *pure*—in the sense of a pure decision—is that which attempts to act outside of experience, language, and history, in short, that which attempts to act outside the reality of human existence. The decision, made by the human sovereign, is therefore always an impure decision and impure exception because it is made from within and in reference to human experience, language, and history.

In discussing this, Taubes makes use of Hans Kelsen who, in 1925, argues a line combining pure theory with strict positivism and is, when the emergency occurs in Weimar, unable to combat despotism because the despotic state is taken to be representative of legal order. To extend Taubes's insight, *pure* theory, whether of law, history, morality, or value, because it does not take account of actual history, has no way to stand against the realities of human history when they occur. On the one hand, the *pure* theorist is left stating an idealism that is too easily, and all to quickly, silenced, overcome, or easily discarded and repressed; more often, under the emergency and despotism, the *pure* theory becomes the claim of state that must be obeyed. That Schmitt saw the dangers of such a *pure* theory, even though he himself became "sucked into" (42) the despotism of the emergency proclaimed in Germany, in fact, speaks to the ongoing and dominating power and control of actual history: none of us is free from experience, from language, from history, and holding onto *pure* theory will not save us, at best it will make us an irrelevance.

This was a central lesson for the left with the collapse of the Marxist bloc post-1989. A *pure* theory resulted in a despotism that became so impure as to cause its own collapse; history overcame *pure* theory; not in a Fukuyama-Hegelian "end of history" but rather more in a Taubean-Schmittean historical apocalypse, where *impure* history overcame an attempted history of *pure* theory. The turn to Schmitt was in effect the turn to *impure* theory to understand why *pure* theory failed, to understand why *impure* history did not collapse whereas a vaunted historical process based, ever increasingly, on *pure* theory, a *pure* theory of history, did.

Other issues identified by Taubes include the problems of violence and the ongoing concerns regarding anti-Semitism and Catholicism (42). Taubes, as a narrativist, decides to tell stories as the way to express his thoughts and, in fact, is always engaged in types of narrative: more than a conversation, less than a monologue, a voice at once personal yet reserved (more expressive of learning and knowledge than of the personal). Regarding the problem of violence, Taubes reports how in two cases philosophy does not want to deal with the question, the problem of violence because it is impure, for violence is too tied into the actors and actions of impure history. The implication is clear, Schmitt is one of the few thinkers who will take the problem of violence seriously, whether from the viewpoint of law or from philosophy, because "law does have a relationship to the problem of violence and power" (43). This relationship is what brings both radical right and radical left together in their use of Schmitt, because Schmitt, in his rejection of the liberalism of Weimar, is one of the very few prepared to take violence and power seriously in a way that takes account of the impurity of human history.

As for anti-Semitism, Taubes notes that this was *only* what they talked about (43) and reports a most challenging confession from Schmitt: "I am a Christian, there is no other way to be a Christian without a touch of anti-Semitism" (44). And yet tied into all this is the wider question, that of the relationship between Germans and Jews from Emancipation, which saw, on the one hand, many German Jews become central figures of, identifiers with, and supporters of high German culture, yet, all too soon, too tragically, the central anti-Semitism of a German Christian identity wherein a combined Catholicism and Lutheranism (along with neopagan Romanticist *Volksgeist*) was easily stoked with horrific results. But Taubes's insight is that liberals were, in the end, not the friends of the Jews in Germany during Emancipation, for, in exchange for Emancipation, Jews had to give up being Jews. Being German was not, as liberals may have thought, an elevated, cosmopolitan identity that Jews could transcend into being. Rather, they could never be a "German of Mosaic confession" (44): in the face of the violence of human history, in the face of impure power and authority, identity is the stuff, the driver, the basis of decisions, and the sovereign exception is often that which revolves around identity.

Both Schmitt and Taubes realize that, in the modern world, in the face of the claim in *The Communist Manifesto* that "all that is solid melts into air, all that is holy profaned," identity—identity of race, of ethnicity, of blood and soil nationalism, of antimodern religion— became the claims of the solid, of that which attempts to holds out against the melting influence of modernity. Specifically for Schmitt it is Catholicism, a right-wing Catholicism Taubes understands as similar to that of Jacques Maritain, wherein they are connected by Leon Bloy. This is because such Catholic thinkers, especially Schmitt, rethink history in and against modernity as containing an antiliberal teleology that brings theology back into philosophy. Taubes seems to be arguing that Schmitt returns historical time to theology, against liberalism, and in this is part of a wider theological refutation of liberalism, including the *Römerbrief* of Karl Barth that similarly sought to overcome the limits and limitations of nineteenth-century German idealism (in Barth's case from a Protestant perspective).

Yet, just as the Marxists similarly critiqued liberalism, there is always the central problem for many that to critique liberalism is to confuse antiliberalism with forms of antidemocratic attitudes. For if liberalism all too often wishes to make humans escape from time and history, to take humans and time and make them *pure*, antiliberalism forgets that democracy is perhaps the best expression of the realities of time and place and impure humanity, because it is precisely so messy and, often, so annoying. The limitations of democracy are precisely the limitations of history and humanity, for like time itself, which is "a duration with a definite ending" (45), is not democracy itself the system that has a built-in duration with a definite ending? Is the problem therefore not democracy, but, as Schmitt, Taubes, and Marxists alike recognize, that of liberal democracy, which seeks to make people, humans, time, and history otherwise than what they are and so attempts to become a type of worst-case combination of salvation drama combined with, too often, a requirement for humans to give up what gives them their identity through the demands of a sovereign liberal state that will always determine who is the exception, and that exception is made up of those who are, who see themselves as, the expression and culmination of liberal history? For all others have to give up to become like liberals, to think like them, to believe, and *not believe*, like them. In short, liberals seek to live, to exist, to govern from and as the sovereign imposing the state of exception, but a state of exception that proclaims a vantage point above and against history and identity. For, as Taubes and Schmitt recognize, as do Marxists from an alternative experience and analysis, liberals and liberalism in effect wish to stop most humans from being time-located, historical humans in the name of idealism and the self-interest of liberals.

Further, when one is located in time, when one exists within a time with definite endings, one is then called upon to act. For "the problem of time is a moral problem" (45), and liberals appear, all too often, to believe problems of time (in history) and of morality can be handled by "discussing without end" (45), whereas antiliberals, who take humanity, history, time, and morals seriously, know that there comes a point when one must act, the parliament must act, the state must act, the sovereign must act, in effect, to restore the awareness that we are limited, impure humans who live in history, who live in time, who are confronted by moral problems that demand a decision, that we exist in a counterweb of identities that are finite as we are finite, and so to put off the decision to a time yet to occur—in short, to postpone the decision to a time without present implication, is amoral.

Morality is important to Schmitt because for him politics is not the domain of a political scientist (he is, we must always remember, a jurist and a philosopher)—and because politics is a degree of intensity—everything can become political. Schmitt reminds us that politics is what we do, what we do within limited time as limited humans, and so anything, within an intensity, is politics, is political when we do it, we practice it: *when we act*. In short, politics is an attitude of and reaction to what can be termed an *event*—especially those events that become matters of identity, of life and death, or if the event is that of an emergency. Therefore what Schmitt offers is way of freeing the historical intensity of the event of the political from the idealism of politics. What Schmitt offers is a new concrete thinking approach to politics, an approach anchored in the events and intensity of real people in history and time, a concrete thinking that Taubes views as similar to that of the Marxist Ernst Bloch (46), an intensity, a concreteness that Taubes traces back to Simmel (46). Then, in a typically Taubean narrative, unable or unwilling to state what it is about Schmitt that fascinates him (despite having earlier stated it was Schmitt's counterrevolutionism), Taubes both deflects and intensifies the question by reading out a letter from Walter Benjamin to Schmitt written in

1930. We need to note that just previously Taubes has linked Schmitt to those other Jewish left-wing thinkers Bloch and Simmel. Now he quotes Benjamin thanking Schmitt for the influence on his own work of Schmitt's writing on sovereignty and the state, and then Taubes concludes by adding his esteem and devotion to that offered by Benjamin. In an instant, Taubes makes us reconsider Benjamin, Taubes, and Schmitt, furthermore making us reconsider how the Frankfurt School might find an unlikely ally in Schmitt (and in this echoing the much later *Telos* debate). For further remembering Schmitt's friend-enemy distinction, *only* the friends-enemies can understand each other and work with and against each other. To understand the concrete politics, the concrete political of the modern world, the antiliberals of the modern world must engage in an ongoing constructive friend-enemy dialectic. For, against Schmitt, against Bloch, against Simmel, against Taubes, against Benjamin, the liberals of Weimar, the legacy of Weimar liberalism, seek to separate us from concrete history, from concrete philosophy, from being able to respond to concrete events. This is what, via Taubes, we can come to describe as the commonality of the problem of the middle. And yet, what eventuates with the problem of the middle is (we must remember) that which Taubes notes, which actually began the friend-enemy relationship of Taubes and Schmitt; for how, wondered Taubes, first privately and then in the letter to Armin Mohler, could such intelligent men, such important philosophers as Heidegger and Schmitt have "flirted" (which is, we are now aware, a completely inadequate understatement) with Nazism? Or, to put it in a different way, is it a response to the failure of the middle, that is, the failure of Weimar liberalism, the failure further of liberalism per se, that can cause a misjudgment of such a "flirtation," a "flirtation" with an antiliberal idealism that *masquerades* as history? Schmitt, in response to the letter, famously anoints Taubes "a Jewish intellectual, who understands more about me than all the rest" (50). Yet what a burden this is. Remember this is very soon after the end of the war, but also at a time (1948) when the planned Israeli constitution was being worked on with the only copy available in the Hebrew University in Jerusalem of Schmitt's *Verfassungslehre*. So there is a tension here, a tension between what Schmitt's political theology offers, especially to those who wish to take theology and politics seriously, who wish to take history and time and the impure actions that eventuate seriously, and the possible implications when the wrong choice is made versus the false attempt of idealism to flee time and history and create a society of the middle. Remember Taubes finds a reception in America, a reception offered by a young Henry Kissinger at Harvard that enables Schmitt to be heard anew because his political theology is presented by a Jew, in America. Taubes, having been "spotted," as he puts it (51), both in Germany because of his letter to Mohler and in America because of his Harvard lecture, gets drawn into what was, for a long time, a one-sided correspondence with Schmitt.

How can we think of this correspondence? Schmitt sends Taubes his writings, with dedications and references and instructions for further readings. Taubes uses the word *pedagogical* (51) for the notes, but perhaps we can read the whole relationship as pedagogical, and, further, Schmitt, sensing perhaps the ideal pupil, the one who will not uncritically accept, but rather engage constructively, also knows that he has discovered the ideal reader, for, as Taubes comments, "he is sure that I have read it" (51). This raises a most interesting and important question: is the friend-enemy the most important and most valuable relationship for any teacher, any writer, any thinker? Are we perhaps most understood by those who are in a friend-enemy relationship, unless of course we are of—and write for, the middle? And, of course, if we are of and for the middle, we are *against* history, *against* time, *against* the concrete experiences of being human in all its political impurity.

Taubes is forced to consider such questions and, in the process, is further forced to consider his response to Schmitt's Nazi "flirtation." For a constant refrain from Taubes is that if he has learned anything he has learned it from Schmitt, and this further leads him to a position in which he cannot be the judge of Schmitt because, as a Jew, he could not be party to the same temptation that Schmitt suffered, because he was "not allowed" to (52). Now it is this phrase, the "not allowed to," that must remind us of that earlier debate on the betrayal of Jews by the German liberals in the nineteenth century as part of Emancipation. Because here Taubes speaks of the tension of what could be termed the German Jew and Jewish German, those who lived the friend-enemy relationship most centrally, most personally—in fact within the core of their emancipated liberal identity. Taubes, in a moment of great confessional honesty, states that in the face of such an event as the Nazi period, to have experienced it on the inside, from within Germany or Austria, as a German, he cannot say that he would not have succumbed and gone mad for at least a couple of years.

In acknowledging this, Taubes rises a further question as to whether it is only, truly, Jews, or at least Jews who takes Taubes's position of not being a judge, who can now, post-1945, really read Schmitt and, to a lesser degree, Heidegger. For all of us who are non-Jews can and, I would argue, *must*, first and foremost, read Schmitt and Heidegger *as if* we too were and are allowed to make their decision or reject it in the face of their temptation. For Schmitt defended, to the end, his decision and statements made during the Nazi state, and Taubes finds himself in a situation whereby he cannot think about it. So, for those of us who are non-Jews, when we read and use Schmitt, this must be not without sharing the possibility of the temptation to which he succumbed. And this is not just because Schmitt, as earlier noted, challenges with what he sees as the necessary anti-Semitism of Christian identity. For, in the West, we who are not or even no longer Christian must also remember we exist in what I term an Italian hermeneutics, somewhere between Ignazio Silone's "Christian without a church and communist without a party"[25] and Benedetto Croce's "we cannot not call ourselves Christian."[26] So a post-Christian or anti-Christian reading, even a Marxist reading of Schmitt, is also linked to the Schmittean problem of Christianity, for Christianity is that which has formed the

culture we exist within—or against. The temptation is part of a further, larger one of what choices we might have made, what choices we
have made or would make in the face of the failure of liberalism. In the
face of such a decision, what choices do we find ourselves facing, and
can we read Schmitt properly without being self-aware of this? For
Schmitt can only be properly read by us today if we too, by reading
him, by making use of him, by engaging in political theology, open
ourselves up to the same temptations and the same possibilities unless
we wish to remain—or become—liberals.

Schmitt and Taubes are, of course, not liberals—and it can be proposed that both of them are, today, most read and used by those who
would not self-identify as liberals: being rather readers from either
a right or left perspective. Instead, we may read Schmitt from a perspective demanded by Taubes that there was never an inevitability in
German history that ended in Hitler, that is, we cannot read German
history, and especially, Taubes emphasizes, we cannot read Weimar
history from the consequence, the standpoint of how it ended. Rather,
and more challengingly, Schmitt writes from one side of what Taubes
identifies as a global civil war, a war between those opposed to liberalism, a war that Taubes claims Schmitt is the only one to have noticed.
Therefore Taubes alerts us further to what we do not want or wish to
be alerted to, and it is Taubes the Jew who reads Schmitt who understands, precisely, yet again, because, while he is likewise antiliberal, he
is not tempted as Schmitt is by the Nazi possibility, but more because
he is not allowed to be so tempted.

But in the midst of this civil war, a civil war brought into startling
clarity by the willingness of the *Telos* left to read and make use of
Schmitt in their battle against liberalism, we must read without false
genealogies of inevitability, genealogies that make us puppets of history and not actors.

For history is lived always open to possibilities, open to consequences, and so decisions must continue to be made, decisions that
are real—very real decisions and not just the unfolding of teleological

inevitability. A central point made here is that liberal democracy—
which allows participation even by those determined to overthrow
it—is not actually in the best interests of the wider society. Liberal
democracy, in short, with its open inclusion, can find itself too easily
overtaken, controlled, and remade by those who are opposed to its
very principles. As the exile Dr. Jochum comments in Malcolm Bradbury's 1965 novel *Stepping Westward*: "Someone once defined liberals
as people who embrace their destroyers. I think protected democracy is proper in a world where there are many destroyers."[27] Or, as
the recipient of this advice, the English "angry young man" novelist
James Walker is forced to consider that "the speciality of liberalism is
the betrayal of the society in which liberalism is permitted to exist."[28]
This is the circumstance in which Weimar Germany found itself—a
circumstance Schmitt sought to oppose. Today, with the resurgence
of ultra-right and ultra-left antidemocratic movements, is a *liberal*
democracy actually the best option—or do we need to limit democracy in order to preserve it? Our answer will depend, as Taubes noted,
on the perspective through which we come to understand the world
(54). Schmitt, as a lawyer, seeks the end of chaos: his aim is to keep
chaos at bay and, via the law, to institute order. Once the state has let
chaos in, the task became how to order the chaotic state. Conversely,
the philosopher and the theologian do not necessarily so fear chaos,
for chaos can be part of a transition to a new situation: chaos can be
the working out of justice, truth, or grace. Schmitt as kathechon was
opposed to the theologian and the philosopher because as the lawyer
he has an investment in the world as it is. Taubes, self-described as
an apocalyptic (54), reads Schmitt as the kathechon and on so doing
again situates himself as the one who Schmitt sees understands more
than anyone else. For what we have presented to us with Schmitt-
Taubes is an extension of the friend-enemy: German-Jewish, lawyer-
theologian, kathechon-apocalyptic. The central irony is that Schmitt's
kathechon becomes participant in a form of apocalypse that unleashes
more chaos than it could ever hope to contain. And yet, as Taubes

ruefully concludes: "here was someone who posed substantive questions, just like Heidegger. That was the fascination" (57).

Taubes, writing elsewhere on the issue between Judaism and Christianity, stresses the importance of "the fundamental issue, which is theological and from which all the social and political questions spring originally."[29] This issue, the difference between the Jewish and Christian religions,[30] sits at the heart of the relationship between Taubes and Schmitt, and their relationship is a reminder of this. How we read their correspondence will, to a greater or lesser degree, also be influenced by this difference, as will our reading of their individual works. Further, the issue between the two (Christian-Jew, Schmitt-Taubes) begins, as Taubes states, from the Christian side,[31] and this is the first instance and origin of what in Schmittean terms is civil war, and it is also therefore the beginning of friend-enemy in Western and Christian thinking, becoming most fully expressed in John's Gospel and by Paul. For the Jewish Christian (to avoid being a heretic) needs the friend-enemy of continuing Judaism, and the Gentile Church, by claiming the new identity that originates *within* Judaism, extends it with an apocalyptic identity that is expressed as the end of the law because of the coming of the Messiah. The Messiah is the sovereign who decides the exception (and its promised future resolution), yet when the Messiah fails to return, the Church becomes sovereign in place of the unreturned Messiah, and it takes on the role of earthly sovereign in his stead. With Schmitt the jurist we see the return of law as normative, in effect an overturning of the sovereign exception of the Messiah, but while the exception of the Messiah was enforced via the new law that was of the Church, now, in the age of Schmitt, even the law of the Church is overturned and superseded by the new sovereign of the state. What we get, as Taubes describes, is opposition to the theological-hierarchical order of the universe by the strongly antitheological basis of secular jurisprudence.[32] However, theological reason and juridical reason both stand strongly opposed to economic reason and also to later technological reason, which is why Schmitt and Taubes as so linked, for both stand opposed to these later forms and governmentality of reason. But here too is the understanding of why, in opposition to economic and technological reason, there has been such a turn to Schmitt—even by the left. For the alternative, as so presented, is to turn to theological reason, and Schmittean juridical reason allows the opposition to theological reason to continue, even as one stands opposed to economic and technological reason. And what we must remember is that theological reason and juridical reason stand as friend-enemy to one another in a way in which economic and technological reason allow no such relationship, for while the theological and the juridical may be engaged with each other in a state of war, in contrast, the economic and the technological are encountered as the expression of apocalypse; there is not civil war with the economic or technological, for they are expressions and visitations of a completely new order.

Is this why, in the face of such apocalypse, we see such a return to political theology, to a position that takes *being human* very seriously, very centrally, a return to a position that grounds us continually in the *impure* realm of history and time? We may not necessarily like either Taubes or Schmitt, but in the face of claims of pure apocalypse from economic and technological reason we must continually state our desire, our need, our willingness, and our necessity to *remain impure*, a claim that in a world increasingly governed by the instruments of pure apocalypse remains "a very rare thing."

TO CARL SCHMITT

CARL SCHMITT

APOCALYPTIC PROPHET OF
THE COUNTERREVOLUTION

I would like to testify to my respect for Carl Schmitt, still a restless spirit in old age—although as a conscious Jew I belong among those whom he has marked as "enemy."

I have never overlooked this axiom of Carl Schmitt. However, what he means by "enemy" is not to be found in his major, clamorous, texts, but rather in his broken confessions, published in 1950 as *Ex Captivitate Salus*.

Carl Schmitt was a jurist, not a theologian; but a legal theorist who entered the scorched earth that theologians had vacated.

Theologians are inclined to define the enemy as something that has to be destroyed. Carl Schmitt sought as a legal theorist to find a way of evading the fatal consequence of this theological definition of the enemy.

But from 1933 to 1938 he made himself the spokesman of National Socialism's Manichaean ideology, which mythologized all Jewry as the destroyer of the Aryan race.

One places oneself in relation to what one considers enmity and how one deals with the "enemy." "Terrible are those who destroy and justify themselves by saying that those who destroy have to be destroyed." This sentence is not merely a judgment upon others, it sits eye to eye with Carl Schmitt's statements on the Jewish question.

In "The Struggle of German Legal Science Against the Jewish Spirit" he swore the allegiance of lawyers to the *Führer,* Adolf Hitler: "By defending myself against the Jews I fight for the Lord."[1] It is an open question whether Carl Schmitt knew even then which "Lord" the *Führer* was fighting for: quite certainly not the "God of Abraham, Isaac and Jacob," nor even "the God of Philosophers" (Pascal).

I was not, however, aware of these lines when, at the age of nineteen, I read for the first time Carl Schmitt's *Political Theology* and had to present a paper on it in a seminar on modern history at the University of Zurich led by Professor Leonhard von Muralt.

The previous year Karl Löwith's *From Hegel to Nietzsche* was published in Zurich;[2] René König, then a lecturer in sociology, drew my attention to Löwith. It was like scales falling from my eyes as I grasped the line that Löwith traced from Hegel via Marx and Kierkegaard to Nietzsche.

Everything I had read or heard so far about the spiritual and intellectual history of the nineteenth century seemed at once stale and irrelevant. It became clear to me that "whoever has tested the depths of European thinking from 1830 to 1848 is as well-prepared as can be for what is today emerging both in East and in West."

My reading of Löwith's new interpretation of what had been forgotten and neglected in pre-1848 Germany made quite clear to me that here was a signpost from which orientation in the global civil war of our generation could be found.

I picked up a reference to Carl Schmitt in Löwith: to chapter 4 of his *Political Theology,* where he demarcates the fronts in the global civil war. The chapter is called "On the Counterrevolutionary Philosophy of the State" and deals succinctly with de Maistre, Bonald, and Donoso Cortés.

The chapter turns on a contrast between Proudhon and Bakunin as advocates of revolution on the one hand and Donoso Cortés as an exponent of the counterrevolution on the other.

Carl Schmitt's reference to the "Satanism" of that time remains unforgettable. This use of "Satanism" is no casual literary metaphor, full of paradox, but instead a solid intellectual principle.

It is an allusion to Baudelaire's unforgettable lines on Satan's elevation to the throne, embodying the inclinations of an entire generation:

> Race of Cain, ascend to heaven
> And cast God down upon the earth!

It was this very significant mid-nineteenth-century intellectual and world-historical opposition that I wanted to bring to the attention of the seminar on "Religion and Politics in the Nineteenth Century."

I linked Carl Schmitt's analysis of that constellation with the line that Löwith had drawn from Hegel to Nietzsche; this seemed to me a kind of philosophical cartography on the basis of which historiography *tel quel,* as currently practiced, can be written. I spoke for forty minutes. There followed a long, almost painful, silence.

The professor then spoke and forestalled any future or possible discussion. First of all he referred to Carl Schmitt, upon whose arguments from the fourth chapter of *Political Theology* I had commented, as an "evil man." Secondly, he rejected as "monstrous and unidimensional" the line running through the first half of the nineteenth century that Karl Löwith proposed. At the end of that seminar my arguments were left in ruins. No other interpretation of the problem I had touched on was proposed, instead one just carried on blindly: from week to week, from topic to topic.

Without intending to, Professor Leonhardt von Muralt had taught me a lesson: that Carl Schmitt was quite right to cite Hobbes— *auctoritas non veritas facit legem* (the law is made by authority, not the truth).

At the time I felt the first seed of doubt about the authority of a professorial university, a seed which took solid root in the course of the 1960s and 1970s. My traumatic memory of that seminar certainly contributed to my opposition to that kind of university during the sixties.

And so it was Carl Schmitt's *Political Theology,* "four chapters on the doctrine of sovereignty," and especially the fourth, "On the Counterrevolutionary Philosophy of the State," that formed the turning point during my years as a student.

It was my hunger for real actors that had driven me to history. I remain, today, sceptical of any philosophy that fails to deal concretely with history. Without history there can be no verification of even the most abstract metaphysical principles. Even as a professor of philosophy I am only interested in history and am in fact of the opinion that history has hardly flourished in the hands of professional historians. The exceptions prove the rule: in Berlin Ernst Nolte and in Bielefeld Reinhart Koselleck—they represent the combination of theory and empiricism that I seek.

It was clear to me right from the start that Carl Schmitt's slim but provocative treatise *Political Theology* was a general onslaught on liberal modernity—whether as a way of life or as a form of knowledge—a critique of the modern mind whose assumptions and basic principles were not sufficiently clear to me. I sought as a student, quite alone and without any guidance apart from the catalogue of the Zurich Central Library, to trace the way in which that treatise had taken shape and discovered that the first three chapters had first appeared under the title "Sociology of the Concept of Sovereignty and Political Theology" in a memorial volume edited by Melchor Palyi: *Hauptprobleme der Soziologie. Erinnerungsgabe für Max Weber,*[3] and that the fourth and final chapter had first been published in the *Archiv für Rechts- und Wirtschaftsphilosophie,* vol. 16 (1922): *Erinnerungsgabe für Max Weber*—I followed this trail.

What connection is there between Max Weber's project and Carl Schmitt's treatise? Who is Carl Schmitt, after all? What is the relation of his own project on "Political Theology" to the work of Max Weber?

If there is one text which conveys the essence of what Max Weber was about it is his "Prefatory Remarks" to the *Gesammelte Aufsätze zur Religionssoziologie.* He opens:

> The child of modern European civilization will inevitably and justifiably approach problems of universal history from the standpoint of the following problematic: What chain of circumstances led to the appearance in the West, of cultural phenomena which—or so at least we like to think—came to have *universal* significance and validity?
>
> Only in the West do we find "*science*" at the stage of development that we today recognize as "valid."[4]

Weber then proceeds through science, art, music, architecture, and the university and then comes to his final point, to the "most fateful force of our modern life, *capitalism.*"[5]

⁂ ⁂ ⁂

Everywhere in the course of his reflections it is the same question: why this rationality was formulated in the Occident, and was only in the Occident formulated in this particular way. Regarding the law, Weber says that "there are embryonic forms in India (Mimamsa School), there is extensive codification, especially in the Near East, and there are plenty of books of laws in India and elsewhere, but outside the West there is an absence of the strictly juridical *schemata* and forms of thought needed for rational jurisprudence found in the Roman law, and in the Western law that grew out of it. Moreover, only the West has a structure like canon law."[6] If I look in the writings of Carl Schmitt for statements where he concretely formulates his own concerns in connection to those of Max Weber's general thesis, I find the following in his confession:

> We are conscious of legal science as a specifically European phenomenon. It is not just a *praxis prudentia,* and not just a craft. It is deeply

embedded in the adventure of Occidental rationalism. In spirit it has
a noble parentage. Its father is reborn Roman Law, and its mother the
Roman Church. Separation from the mother was finally completed
after centuries of hard struggle during the era of confessional civil
wars. The child cleaved to its father, Roman Law, and left its mother's
home. It sought a new home, and found it in the state. This new home
was in a principality, a renaissance or a baroque palace. Jurists were
proud of themselves, and felt far superior to theologians.[7]

I cannot here cite any more such passages, but think I have presented
enough material to make quite clear that this represents a central statement of Carl Schmitt's self-understanding. He here shows himself to
be a legitimate, and not an illegitimate, son of Max Weber. In these
paragraph of his short book *Ex Captivitate Salus,* Carl Schmitt talks
of how, during his imprisonment and the subsequent period—a time
when, as was then usual, he was "questioned" and supposed to sub-
mit to democratic reeducation—he reflected on the significance of
medieval clerics, on their doctrine of just war and just resistance to
tyranny: "They forged sentences of such indestructible actuality that
one can quote them only in Latin, as with the marvellous chapter
titles in Policratius: *Tyrannum licet adulari* (the tyrant is to be wor-
shipped), *tyrannum licet decipere* (the tyrant is to be deceived), *tyrannum licet occidere* (the tyrant is to be struck down)." I think that these
three stages can be understood as an allegory of Carl Schmitt's history
under the banner of National Socialist tyranny. To begin with adula-
tion, then deception by ambiguous distantiation, and finally connection to groups who contemplate the rejection of the regime.

During the crisis of 1848 Donoso Cortés had, almost a century previously, placed decision over discussion and coined the aphorism that
the liberal bourgeoisie was a *clasa discutidora,* a "discussing class." This
provided Carl Schmitt with the sharpest of weapons when, a year after
the publication of *Political Theology,* he identified *Die geistesgeschichtliche Lage des heutigen Parlamentarismus,*[8] a polemic that resonated

not only through the ongoing crisis of the Weimar Republic, but one that during the 1960s became a vade mecum for an intelligentsia of the left.

It is true that since the 1960s one can talk of a leftist Schmitt reception, but in fact there was already a leftist reception during the Weimar period. One name that can be mentioned here is that of Otto Kirchheimer, jurist and student of Schmitt and a member of the Institute for Social Research in Frankfurt. I am not myself trained in law, and I read and understood *Political Theology* as a politico-theological treatise, and not primarily as a legal one.

The first few lines of the third chapter run as follows:

> All significant concepts of the modern theory of the state are secularized theological concepts not only because of their historical development—in which they were transferred from theology to the theory of the state, whereby, for example, the omnipotent God became the omnipotent lawgiver—but also because of their systematic structure, the recognition of which is necessary for a sociological consideration of these concepts. The state of exception in jurisprudence is analogous to the miracle in theology. Only by being aware of this analogy can we appreciate the manner in which the philosophical idea of the state developed over the last few centuries.[9]

I had quickly come to see Carl Schmitt as an incarnation of Dostoevsky's Grand Inquisitor.[10] During a stormy conversation at Plettenberg in 1980 Carl Schmitt told me that anyone who failed to see that the Grand Inquisitor was right about the sentimentality of Jesuitical piety had grasped neither what a Church was for, nor what Dostoevsky—contrary to his own conviction—had "really conveyed, compelled by the sheer force of the way in which he posed the problem."

I always read Carl Schmitt with interest, often captivated by his intellectual brilliance and pithy style. But in every word I sensed something alien to me, the kind of fear and anxiety one has before a storm, an anxiety that lies concealed in the secularized messianic dart of Marxism. Carl Schmitt seemed to me to be the Grand Inquisitor of all heretics.

To talk of Carl Schmitt also meant to talk of Carl Schmitt the literary stylist. His statements are striking and incisive: "Sovereign is he who decides on the exception"[11] or "All significant concepts of the modern theory of the state are secularized theological concepts."[12] I cite here just these two, which introduce the first and the third chapters of *Political Theology* and set up the subsequent course his argument takes. As Günter Maschke noted in his obituary, his style combines "rational incisiveness" with "fevered, apocalyptic" elements.[13] Carl Schmitt can be read and understood both as a jurist and as an apocalyptic prophet of the counterrevolution. Carl Schmitt addressed me in terms of the latter. As an apocalyptic spirit I felt and still feel close to him. And we follow common paths, even as we draw contrary conclusions.

In 1948 I went to New York and stumbled upon part of the anonymous career of Carl Schmitt's *Political Theology*, in particular of its fourth chapter, "On the Counterrevolutionary Philosophy of the State," which is an arcane piece of the intellectual history of the present.

The fourth chapter of Albert Salomon's *Tyranny of Progress* is a work entirely in the spirit of the fourth chapter of *Political Theology*.[14] So much is plain to any reader from a comparison of p. 62 of Salomon's book with p. 63 of Schmitt's. In each case a contrast is being drawn between Proudhon/Bakunin on the one hand and Donoso Cortés on the other.

I do not mention this filiation between Schmitt and Salomon so that I might accuse the latter of plagiarism. I am instead more interested in Carl Schmitt's influence in the U.S. For this chapter from Salomon's book also appeared in the volume published following the 1941 Conference on Science, Philosophy and Religion at Columbia University.[15] It was the only contribution that was not original, having been reprinted from the journal *Social Research,* edited by the Graduate Faculty of the New School for Social Research.[16] The conference itself had been initiated by the Jewish Theological Seminary in New York, whose president was Louis Finkelstein.

※ ※ ※

Carl Schmitt's attempt to define the theology of the counterrevolution was also adopted as the ideology of a new academic conservatism, propagated throughout the United States by the institution of Conservative Judaism. This connection would need studying if ever an intellectual history of ideology in the U.S. of the early 1940s were written.

During these years there was an exodus of some of the most gifted assistant professors from Columbia University, which at the time was a bulwark of American pragmatisim. Richard McKeon and Mortimer Adler left New York for Chicago, for the university that Robert M. Hutchins had reformed.

His reform can be summed up as the abolition of football and the introduction of Thomism. Jacques Maritain and Leo Strauss directed the Committee on Social Thought.

It is in this context that we should see the repristination and anonymous career of Schmitt and his *Political Theology,* and its dark and sombre fourth chapter, "On the Counterrevolutionary Philosophy of the State."

※ ※ ※

In 1949 I went to Jerusalem as a Research Fellow with the Warburg Prize; Gershom Sholem, kabbalist and friend of Walter Benjamin, was my patron. Not only was Jerusalem a divided city in the 1940s and 1950s, but the Hebrew University had been exiled from Mount Scopus and was located in a monastery in the city center. The great library was locked up on Mount Scopus, where an Israeli guard changed every fortnight under the supervision of the United Nations.

Contrary to the terms of the official truce, which said that nothing could be taken from Mount Scopus into the city, and nothing from the city to Mount Scopus, the decree was circumvented with the help of members of the guard who, when they came back to the city, filled their trousers and bags with books that the university library had labeled "urgent."

So it came about that, as a novice, I was to give lectures on the philosophy of the seventeenth century. I went to the library director and told him of my problem. For a lecture on Descartes I needed a historical and philosophical sketch of the term *law* in both its natural scientific and juridico-theological senses.

The differing conceptions that came together in the term *Gesetz* had to be identified more exactly. The only source that could help me deal with this problem was Carl Schmitt's *Verfassungslehre,* which dealt with the problem of *nomos/lex/Gesetz.*

The chief librarian listened carefully, but explained that he was powerless to speed the book ordering process. It could take two or three months before I got hold of the book. This was little help, since in three months the semester would be over.

You can imagine how surprised I was when, three weeks later, just before the beginning of the semester, I was called to the library and was able to pick up a copy of Schmitt's *Verfassungslehre.* The chief librarian quickly explained that I should not get any big ideas; the day after I had put in a request for the *Verfassungslehre* they had received an urgent call from the Ministry of Justice: the minister of justice, Pinchas Rosen (formerly Rosenblüth), needed Schmitt's *Verfassungslehre* so that he could deal with some difficult problems in the drafting of a constitution for the state of Israel. The book was therefore immediately brought from Mount Scopus and had now arrived in the library on its return journey, where my urgent request had been kept against an "opportune moment."

There is a subsequent European and American history to this. I must admit to being more bemused than taken with the idea that the constitution of the State of Israel (a constitution which fortunately still does not exist) would be drafted using Schmitt's *Verfassungslehre* as a guide.

I wrote about this to my "Swiss" school friend Armin Mohler and added to it a reflection on the problem of the Fascist intelligentsia. I wrote something like: for me, Martin Heidegger and Carl Schmitt are the most significant exponents of German intellect from the later 1920s and early 1930s. That both involved themselves with the Hitler regime presents me with a problem that I cannot resolve by appealing to the inner bastard of Nazism. I mentioned also that both came from a Catholic background, just like Hitler and Goebbels actually.

At the time, between 1949 and 1952, Armin Mohler was the secretary of Ernst Jünger. Carl Schmitt visited Ernst Jünger, heard about the letter and the story, got Armin Mohler to give him a copy of the letter,[17] which he then sent to his friends (as he tended to do) together with a note in which he wrote about this letter from a Jewish intellectual, to whom he attributed a greater understanding of Carl Schmitt than that of many long-standing colleagues.

But I had no idea of what was happening in the new Federal Republic. Returning from Jerusalem to the U.S., I was looking for an academic appointment. Part of that process involves presenting yourself repeatedly to meetings more officious than official.

So it happened that I presented to a seminar on political theory at Harvard some ideas on the coincidence of political and religious symbolism, ideas that were linked to Carl Schmitt. Since there was at the time no "leftist" political theology, I went beyond this association, in that instead of presenting the apocalypse of the counterrevolution I presented the apocalypse of the revolution, although free from the illusions of messianic Marxists like Ernst Bloch and Walter Benjamin.

Their mystic tenor in Marxism did not bother me, since I have too much respect for the Marxist system of coordinates in which, it seems to me, there is no place for religious experience. The critique of ideologies corrodes and consumes all religious substance.

I appreciate the approach taken by Ernst Bloch and Walter Benjamin—it is replicated on a trivial level in left Catholic and left Protestant circles, and flourishes today in the Christianity of popular churches in Latin America.

But, despite the great intellectual efforts with concept and image on the part of Bloch and Benjamin, there remains a hiatus that cannot be mastered by Marxism.

※ ※ ※

Then, and still today, I have been seeking a new concept of time and a new experience of history opened up by Christianity as an eschatology—itself the fruit and consequence of the apocalypse of the first pre-Christian century.

Carl Schmitt, expressing his love of the Roman Church and also antiapocalyptic emotion, had some sense of this in speaking of the "Christian Empire as the restrainer (*Katechon*) of the Antichrist":

> "Empire" in this sense meant the historical power to *restrain* the appearance of the Antichrist and the end of the present eon; it was a power that withholds (*qui tenet*), as the Apostle Paul said in Second Letter to the Thessalonians [2 Thessalonians 2:6]. This idea of empire can be documented in many quotations of the church fathers, in utterances of German monks in the Frankish and Ottonian ages—above all, in Haimo of Halberstadt's commentary on the Second Letter to the Thessalonians, and in Adso's letter to Queen Gerberga, as well as in Otto of Freising's utterances and in other evidence until the end of the Middle Ages. This provides a sense of an historical epoch. The empire of the Christian Middle Ages lasted only as long as the idea of the *katechon* was alive.

I do not believe that any historical belief other than *katechon* would have been possible for the original Christian faith. The belief that a restrainer holds back the end of the world provides the only bridge between the notion of an eschatological paralysis of all human events and a tremendous historical monolith that of the Christian empire of the German kings.[18]

Carl Schmitt thinks apocalyptically, but from above, from the powers that be; I think from the bottom up. Common to us both is the experience of time and history as a delimited respite, as a term or even a last respite. Originally that was also a Christian experience of history.

The Kat-echon, the restrainer that Schmitt contemplates, is already an early sign of how the Christian experience of the End of the World was domesticated and came to an arrangement with the world and its powers.

Of course, even history as a respite can be interpreted in different ways and lose its acuity, simply wear out.[19] Only through the experience of the end of history does it become that one-way street represented by Occidental history, for us at any rate.

I presented these heretical ideas to a group headed by Henry Kissinger, major domo to a Professor Y. Elliot, about whom I knew nothing more than that Henry had been his assistant for a long time. After my presentation, a young German Fulbright student approached me: it was, he said, interesting and exciting to listen in Harvard to a close friend of Carl Schmitt. "What, me a friend of Carl Schmitt? I am a Jew and elevated into the arch-enemy of Carl Schmitt." To which Hans-Joachim Arndt, later professor for political science in Heidelberg, said: "'But I know your letter to Carl Schmitt!" "What letter was that?" I asked, but it soon became clear to me that it must involve my letter to Armin Mohler, which had subsequently done the rounds of the Federal Republic. Hans-Joachim Arndt took my address to Plettenberg and from then on I occasionally received offprints and signed books that promoted reflection and thought. I read every line, of that Carl Schmitt could be certain. But I never replied. Ultimately there was something unresolved between us that was not insignificant, something neither you nor I could ignore: our still fragile relationship was overshadowed by an active anti-Semitism (and it was a relationship, since I did not refuse mail from him; it was simply that I never responded).

A decade later I came to Berlin. In 1967 Alexander Kojève was a visiting fellow of our institute. He gave a lecture, and you could have heard a pin drop when his listeners heard that history had now come to an end and could only be "recapitulated" in the form of a fictive "as if." These were ideas that met considerable resistance and moral disgust among adherents of progress and futurology. Kojève was notoriously fond of shock effects, renowned for enigmatic rhetoric, for statements that, spoken *ex cathedra,* were nonetheless presented simply as commentary to Hegel's *Philosophy of the Spirit.*

In 1967 Kojève was at the Hotel Berliner am Dianasee surrounded by the leading student "rebels," Dutschke & Co., to whom he said, among other things, that the most important thing for them as student leaders to do would be—to learn Greek. The leaders of the SDS stood there quite perplexed. They had been ready for anything except that.

I was looking after Kojève, and he soon left Berlin. I asked where he was off to now (he had arrived directly from Beijing). His answer: to Plettenberg.

I was stunned, although I had to some extent gotten used to surprises with Kojève. He went on: where else in Germany could one go? Carl Schmitt was after all the only person worth talking to. I felt a twinge of jealousy. For I had failed to go and visit Carl Schmitt and I somehow envied Kojève the ease with which he was able to do so.

But Kojève was after all a Russian, originally Kojevnikov; he had been supervised by Jaspers in Heidelberg with a dissertation on Vladimir Soloviev, the "Russian Hegel," and friend of Dostoevsky, hence a part of an apocalyptic nation just as Carl Schmitt was a part of a

German empire with claims on salvation. By contrast, I was the son of a people that was really chosen by God, a condition that aroused the envy of exactly that apocalyptic nation, an envy that set phantasms to work and disputed the right to life of the truly chosen people.

I have absolutely no doubt that the Jewish problem tormented Schmitt for the whole of his life, that 1936 was merely a "timely" opportunity to take a stand on a problem that, for him, had quite other depths. He was a Christian, and of the people who looked enviously upon those who "are Israelites; to whom pertaineth the adoption, and the glory, and the covenants, and the giving of the law, and the service of God, and the promises; Whose are the fathers, and of whom as concerning the flesh Christ came."[20]

Christianity was for Schmitt always "Judaism for the people," against whose power he was ever ready to rise up. But he saw more deeply how vain such a "protest" against God and history would be.

Much later, very late, much too late, I decided to change trains in Dortmund on one of my routine trips to the nineteenth-century capital and take a train to the Sauerland.[21]

※ ※ ※

In Plettenberg I had the most violent discussions that I have ever had in the German language. It was basically about historiography forced into a mythical construction. It is a professional preconception that mythic images or mystic terminology represent indistinct oracles, pliable and submissive to any will, while the scientific language of positivism owns the rights to truth. There can be nothing further removed from reality than this historical preconception. In the struggle against historism, Carl Schmitt knew himself to be at one with Walter Benjamin or, more exactly, Benjamin knew himself to be at one with Schmitt.

This is one of the darkest chapters in the history of the leftist intelligentsia, but quite certainly one of the most promising constellations of the Weimar republic. Gershom Scholem has drawn attention to

the fact that Walter Benjamin had, even as a historical materialist—
the sole exception here is Bert Brecht—intensively studied so-called
reactionary authors such as Proust, Green, Jouhandeau, Baudelaire,
and George.

It is quite plain, and cannot even be denied by the Frankfurt Institute, that Walter Benjamin made an intensive study of Carl Schmitt.
Benjamin's *Origin of German Tragic Drama,* not a materialist but certainly a dialectical work, contains many references to Carl Schmitt. Its
entire elaboration of the function of the sovereign in baroque drama is
transposed from Schmitt's *Political Theology.* Benjamin demonstrates
that himself in his references.

※ ※ ※

In a *curriculum vitae* written around 1930 Benjamin identifies the art
historian Alois Riegl as the methodological model for his work as well
as "the contemporary efforts of Carl Schmitt, whose analysis of political formations essays an analogous attempt at integrating phenomena
only superficially capable of isolation by domain."

Besides that there is a letter from Benjamin to Schmitt that has
been omitted from the published edition of his correspondence. It
turns out to be a ticking bomb that comprehensively shatters our pre-
conceptions regarding the intellectual history of the Weimar period.
The letter comes not from the early years, but from the time of crisis:
December 1930.

> Dear Professor,
>
> In the next few days you will receive my book *Ursprung
> des deutschen Trauerspiels* from the publisher. I write these
> lines not only to tell you this but also to express my pleasure
> that I might, at the prompting of Albert Salomon, send it
> to you. You will quickly notice how much the book owes to

your treatment of sovereignty in the seventeenth century. Perhaps I might go beyond that and say that I have also found in your later works, particularly *Die Diktatur,* a confirmation of my working methods as a philosopher of art deriving from your own approach to the philosophy of the state. If your reading of my book assists in your understanding this feeling, then my intention in sending it to you is fulfilled.

Expressing my special esteem, your devoted

Walter Benjamin.

I cannot here pursue the comparison that Benjamin makes. I will close by quoting Benjamin's eighth historical-philosophical thesis. In some respects this represents Benjamin's legacy, and here he sees eye to eye with Carl Schmitt: "The tradition of the oppressed teaches us that the 'state of exception' in which we live has become the rule. We have to find a concept of history corresponding to this. Then our task will come to be the creation of a real 'state of exception'; and in this our position in the struggle against fascism will improve." Schmitt's fundamental vocabulary is here introduced by Benjamin, made use of, and so transformed into its opposite. Carl Schmitt's conception of the "state of exception" is dictatorial, dictated from above; in Benjamin it becomes a doctrine in the tradition of the oppressed. "Contemporaneity," a monstrous abbreviation of a messianic period, defines the experience of history on the part of both Benjamin and Schmitt; both involve a mystic conception of history whose principal teaching relates the sacred order to the profane. But the profane cannot be constructed upon the idea of God's empire. This is why theocracy did not, for Benjamin, Schmitt, and Bloch, have a political meaning, but solely a religious significance.

If I understand anything at all of the mystical historical construction that Benjamin here constructs with one eye on Schmitt's theses, then this: what is superficially a process of secularization, of desacralization, the dedeification of public life, a process of step-by-step neutralization right up to the "value freedom" of science as an index of a techno-industrial form of life; this process also has an inner face that testifies to the freedom of God's children (as in the letters of St. Paul), hence an expression of a reformation that is nearing its completion.

Despite all his wanderings, the flux of his theory and his life, I still have a strong impression of Carl Schmitt, one best expressed by Hugo Ball in 1924, in the first paragraph of his review of *Political Theology* in the periodical *Hochland:*

> Carl Schmitt is one of the few German scholars who can face up to the professional dangers of a contemporary professorial position. I am not here claiming that he is the first to have mastered and initiated this new German scholarly type. If the writings of this professor (not to say confessor) only served to allow us to recognise and study the catholic (in its universal, rather than religious, sense) physiognomy of its author, that would be quite enough to secure them a very prominent place. In his essay "On the Ideal" Chesterton once said that it was not some great practical man that was needed to heal our confused and terrible times, but a great ideologist. "A practical man means a man accustomed to mere daily practice, to the way things commonly work. When things will not work, you must have the thinker, the man who has some doctrine about why they work at all. It is wrong to fiddle while Rome is burning; but it is quite right to study the theory of hydraulics while Rome is burning."[22] Carl Schmitt belongs to those who "study the theory of hydraulics"; he is an ideologue of singular conviction; and one can also claim that he will help elevate this word, since Bismarck's time with an evil reputation among Germans, once more to respectability [*sic!* J. T.].

LETTER TO ARMIN MOHLER

14 February 1952

Dear Armin,

   Your lines really pleased me, for I thought that you might have resented my criticism. If I am not wrong, last time I wrote it was on airmail paper, and as I ran out of space I had just finished the "negative" part. . . . So it is good that you have taken the criticism in such a friendly way.

   In medias res: Carl Schmitt is (besides Heidegger) *the* intellectual potential who stands head and shoulders above all intellectual scribbling. There is no doubt about that. (By the way: Israel's minister of justice, working on constitutional matters, put in an *urgent* request at the University Library for Schmitt's *Verfassungslehre*. When it became plain that the book was "up there," i.e., on Mount Scopus, to which we have no access, it was specially fetched by soldiers—soldiers who, under UN protection, drive through "enemy lines" every fortnight to guard the university buildings and the hospital, which stand empty.) It remains a problem for me that both C. S. and M. H. welcomed the National Socialist "revolution" and went along with it and it remains a problem for me that I cannot just dismiss by using catchwords such as vile, swinish. In front of me there is a note on C. S.'s essay "Der Führer schützt das Recht" (*Deutsche Juristen Zeitung*, 1934), and I don't know what to do with it. What was so "seductive" about National Socialism? Was the breakdown of the liberal-humanist world reason enough to rush into the arms of these lemures?[1] A short essay reached Jerusalem (not sent to me unfortunately, but to an "opponent" of the Germans): *Ex Captivitate Salus.* Others thought it "disgusting": too little confession of guilt, pusillanimous. To me it seemed a shocking account, while not clarifying everything, it did permit a profound glimpse into the soul; never have I read such an intimate but so noble (and also truthful) account, a reckoning with oneself, by one of our generation. If only M. H. had had the courage to be so open, following his Rectoral Address of 1933, and more . . . relationship to Husserl, article in the student newspaper (have you ever seen this? Could I have a copy? Buber told me that in 1947 Löwith wrote about this in *Les Temps Modernes*).[2] Better that he had told German youth to stay where they were, that would have been a better path than the "field-paths" (I could not at first believe that this meditation, marinated à la Stifter,[3] came from M. H. and assumed that it was some kind of lexical resemblance when I saw the essay in the Catholic journal *Wort und Wahrheit.* But Buber told me: Taubes, you know *Sein und Zeit,* you don't know H.—and he was right).

But that brings us back to C. S. Taking account of all that, I still have trouble with *Der Nomos der Erde.* Given the extent of the topic, given that the Eurocentrism of international law is on the wane (only international law???), that the old "*nomos* of the world" is in decline, given that human thought has to "turn once more to the elementary

order of terrestrial existence"—then it is an open question
whether the book is a match for the theme that it addresses,
as well as the "contemporary situation," both of which are
truly "overwhelming." Why? The reference to a new *nomos*
recalls (is meant to recall?) John 13:34,[4] recalls ἐντολήν
καινήν δίδωμί—C. S. sees the parallel, for he sees that "this
singular, almighty, great parallel between the present and
the transitional epoch," a parallel that should not be taken
for one of the numerous historical parallels with which the
history books teem. But can the new *nomos* of the earth be
measured against that of Christ? I know the next objection
(it is obvious!): well, how can you make a comparison like
"that"! John 13:34 belongs to theology; the authority of
jurisprudence does not run that far! But then the doctrine
of law still owes an answer for the "decisive case," that
is, an answer to the question of the fate of man in the
constellation of tyranny, in the total rule by force—and,
following that, an answer to all succeeding decisive cases.
The conclusion that follows from this—that state law stops
here—had already been drawn by C. S. himself in the 1933
preface to *Political Theology.* I don't need to write down
the lines. The foreign policy "variants" of international
law stand and fall with the question what is just law. Now
C. S. has to take a position on this, after the tyranny, to
put it mildly. Is it only for others (*das Ausland*) to collect
"material" on concentration camps and gas chambers, or
is it rather a task for those with an inner connection to
Germany to confront what has been done in the name
of the German people and explain, if at all possible, what
happened and why? That would be rather more of a match
for the "immensity of the theme" of the new *nomos* of
the earth! Earth and sea—without men they remain just
"material" (not really even "material"). If humanism has run

dry (from Plato to Nietzsche, as Heidegger says), that only means that the question of man is posed in a more radical fashion than humanism could ever dream of. And who decides on the division of domains: theology, jurisprudence, etc. . . . ? The university curriculum, the running of a liberal society? What is there today that is not "theology" (apart from theological claptrap)? Is Ernst Jünger less a "theologian" than Bultmann or Brunner?[5] Kafka less so than Karl Barth? And of course the question of the law today must be posed "theologically": i.e., it has to be asked: what does the law look like, given that atheism is our fate? Does the Occident have to suffocate in blood and madness in the absence of sacred law, or are we able, "on the basis of the worldly, mortal situation of man," to tell right from wrong (*Recht und Unrecht scheiden*)? The present situation is far more difficult than in the transitional epoch, since, despite the current "spike" on the religious bourse (no more than commotion associated with a restoration!), we very much have to *live* in a post-Christian manner (but the problems are not so "simple" as St. Peter and E. J. imagined. The "minimum" of metaphysics does not mean "less," but more "elementary" in matters metaphysical).

For the "time being" (for the last year and a half), what interests me are the problems of political theology exemplified by Maimonides. The problem of political theology is a bulls-eye (does the term come from C. S.?) of which thus far no use at all has been made. Political theology is perhaps a "cross" for all theology to bear; can it deal with it? Christianity (St. Augustine) has turned down the problem (together with chiliasm, antinomianism—this still lurks in the Christian consciousness, but with a bad conscience). Judaism "is" political theology—that is its "cross," since theology is certainly not exhausted by dividing it up "politically." For the law is not the first and the last, because there are "even" relations between man and man that "exceed," "infringe" the law—love, pity, forgiveness (not at all "sentimental," but "real"). I could not go one step further in my poor and often crooked life (and I have no idea how to go one step further) without holding fast to "these three," and that always leads me, against my "will," to St. Paul.

Heartfelt greetings,

Jacob

APPENDIX

FOUR PASSAGES FROM **LETTERS OF CARL SCHMITT** TO **ARMIN MOHLER**

14 APRIL 1952

The letter from Jacob Taubes that I have had copied is quite astonishing, a major document. I have shown it to a few acquaintances of good judgment; all of them were very moved by it. An old, very cultured, and experienced journalist from the time of the old monarchy (Rudolf Fischer) said after reading it: Bring that Jew here! I could tell you a great deal more of the effect of this letter. But I am sure that he has not read *Nomos der Erde*, for otherwise he would have gone into the quote from St. John on p. 33. I would really like to send him all three publications, but not directly from me. Should I do it in your name? The term "political theology" really is one that I coined . . .

18 JULY 1952

You are right that one should not make so free with letters. But it is unfortunately the case that there is today no public realm, and the most important things are said in letters. A fantastic example is the letter of Jacob Taubes. I have shown it to several people, and all of them were deeply moved by it, in particular by what it says of the condition of theology . . .

6 JULY 1958

In July or August I would like to come to see you in Paris to discuss the thousand items that have piled up here in the past few years. I would also like to see mutual friends, especially Ernsy Kern, and meet Jacob Taubes...

14 AUGUST 1958

Taubes is right: today everything is theology, with the exception of what the theologians talk about...

LETTER TO CARL SCHMITT

Maison des Sciences des Hommes, Paris, 18 September 1979

Dear Herr Schmitt,

Let me thank you once again for your cordial reception, indeed, reception of a friend; for your patience and the openness with which you talked of the failures in the long life of a legist. But such failures, if I might say, using a phrase that still rings in my ears from my time as a student, can be "an incomparable political teacher."[1]

Simply as an arch-Jew I hesitate to burn my bridges. Because in all the unspeakable horror we were spared one thing. We had no choice: Hitler made us into absolute enemies. And there was no choice in this, nor any judgment, certainly not about others. But this does not mean that I am not concerned to understand what "really" happened (not at all in the historical sense, but rather in the eschatological aspect of the disaster)—how the points were set for catastrophe (ours *and* yours). Which brings us to the topic of political theology, to Peterson's "Parthian assault."

The worthy and dignified work of the Heidelberg scholar[2] has, as I already suggested to you, only made the problem clearer. All that is important is in *Politische Theologie II*,[3] although in the form of an attack on Peterson—without noticing that Peterson's "weak point" is really his strength, his actuality—1935.[4]

Dedicated to St. Augustine, introduced with a prayer that this church father should help us today in the midst of "transitional times" (I cite from memory), closed with a reference to Carl Schmitt's *Political Theology*—a final comment exiled to the footnotes regarding the theological impossibility of a political theology—this quite unique introduction and termination was (and is) directed straight at you. For such an important stylist as Peterson one must pay attention not only to what he often repeats, something that can and should be registered through use of a computer, but in particular to something that occurs just once, his "leap" (from Eusebius to Augustine). As if "Professor" Erik Peterson had not himself "noticed," and could not, if he had so wished, prepare himself better as an academic!

You yourself have established that the term *Führer* is unique, as is the reference to "Christian ideology" for Eusebius's *theologumenon*. Also astonishing is the reference to *Civitas Dei* III.30, which has nothing "historical," but which in 1935 was shockingly contemporary: *caecus atque improvidus futurorum*, a coded warning to you—which you never received. You have had no better friend than Peterson to put you on the path to the Christian Church. "True are the wounds that the arrow of a friend inflicts" (in Hebrew abbreviated to *ne'emanim pizei ohev*) it says somewhere in Psalms (there is no Bible to hand here at the Maison). Peterson's arrow is no Parthian arrow, but a Christian one.

Although I in no respect take lightly the fact that the Nazi program talked of "positive Christianity" and took this "seriously" with regard both to Catholicism and Protestantism (wanted to take seriously, and could do: Hitler and Goebbels never left the "church," and, if I am right, they paid their church tax right up to the end!),[5] the "race question" was introduced and adumbrated according to a political "theozoology" (not my expression, but Liebenfels's, who intended it "positively" and gave the term to Hitler) that had to be heard. Or not? I cannot hear that from the interior of the Church . . . I only wish to learn how to "understand" why the boundary was not thought to be here, despite Romans 13.

At the moment I read dutifully through a recent Hobbes commentary and cannot get over how it constantly misses the point—Hobbes left no room for doubt that *Leviathan* deals with the commonwealth first in terms of an ecclesiastical relationship and then as a civil one. So I have to go back to your forty-year-old small book on Leviathan as a symbol and feel sorry for scientific progress. I am not sure whether one should read Hobbes *à la lettre* to a greater extent than you propose. Why should *Leviathan* be treated only as a "literary insight"? Hobbes is in deadly earnest when he talks of the great Leviathan as that "mortal God"—and that is the real point, peace and defense are owed "under the mortal God." And that is why "that Jesus is the Christ" is no cliché, but a recurring statement. And that is also why the machinery of state is no *perpetuam mobile,* a Thousand-Year *Reich,* without end, but mortal, a fragile equilibrium both within and without, always capable of failure. It was not the "first liberal Jew"[6] who discovered this point of rupture, but the Apostle Paul (of whom the "first liberal Jew" "thought extremely highly"), to whom I turn in transitional times—he had distinguished inside from outside even for "the political." Without such a distinction we are at the mercy of throne and powers that, in a "monistic" cosmos, have no sense of a hereafter. One can argue over the boundary between the spiritual and the worldly, and this boundary will constantly be redrawn (an everlasting task of political theology), but if this distinction is neglected, then we breathe our last (Occidental) breath—that goes for Thomas Hobbes too, who always distinguishes ecclesiastical from civil power. Your reference to Barion's remark in the *Savigny Zeitschrift* stands in for whole libraries of Hobbes "commentary."[7] I am going to Zurich, where the material I need is easier to find (here I can't track down either Barion or Kempf) and want to use this reference (which represents a significantly more precise formulation than that of your little book on Hobbes) to get started with the Hobbes-Spinoza lecture—given to students whose guidance comes at best from Strauss,[8] at worst from Macpherson.[9] The lecture is a risk given the marxisant atmosphere, and it has been deliberately marked "for advanced students only" and so distinct from the market for the philosophy students we serve in the institute, and the public will very likely be excluded—which can only work in its favor.

Please do not be *iam frustra doces* Carl Schmitt on account of diversions and failures (or involving poor Julius Stahl, whom I surreptitiously "admire"). Perhaps the right moment will come when we can discuss the theology of Romans 9–11, which I find the most important political theology, whether Jewish or Christian.[10] There can be found the word *enemy* (Romans 11:28) in an absolute sense that seems to me the most promising of all starting points, coupled with *loved*. That these chapters were "at stake" in 1935 (and remains so in 1978)—Peterson, your (apparent)

critic and (actual) best friend, knew that. And this marks
the clearest separation between him and the existentialism
of his most important contemporary in matters of New
Testament exegesis, Rudolf Bultmann. Through Peterson
many will still find their way to Plettenberg—will have
to do so.

With friendly greetings,

Yours, Jacob Taubes

EXTRACT FROM A DISPUTE ABOUT CARL SCHMITT

PARIS, 1986

Herr Berding, you have not made it very easy for me, since, by referring to "Der Führer schützt das Recht"[1] and "Die deutsche Rechtswissenschaft im Kampf gegen den jüdischen Geist,"[2] you have already directed the discussion down a one-way street, and so you compel me, if I understand this discussion properly, to begin with a response to that. The kind of discussion that we propose is not an easy one, and I approach it with mixed feelings, although mixed in a positive sense: that I am in fact happy for the director of this institute to have already used the word *dispute*. So there are no misunderstandings here, we certainly do not want to end up in each others' arms, to say that ultimately we meant the same thing but used different words—that is all a matter of consensus, we are instead trying to mark out our differences. But, on the other hand, trying to do so introduces something of the suspense of the circus to a conference, as someone said this morning over breakfast—and especially here in Paris, bearing in mind the recent Franco-German meeting—and that makes me rather anxious. We have therefore to steer between marking our differences and avoiding extravagance. Neither of us are trapeze artists, and we have known each other for many years. If I might add to that, Professor Sontheimer was a colleague of mine in Berlin, but he moved from Berlin to Munich, and, as you know, the distance between Berlin and Munich is also a spiritual one. I am no German, but I do think that it is like that for Germans: Munich always opposed Prussia, and Humboldt's great university reform was always viewed with disquiet from Munich. You know too that when the great Hegelian wave was over (in our institute we are of course successors to Hegel) Schelling was appointed from Munich to finish off the Hegelian dragon. There is a Berlin-Munich syndrome: let's say, for instance, we tried to appoint Habermas, while you in Munich turned him down as an honorary professor. . . . But let's get to the point.

You can see that I am cast here as an apologist for Carl Schmitt. I don't accept this role. I face a very difficult problem: it is no secret that I am and am conscious of being Jewish, am an *Erzjude,* and this involves some problems for me in German lands. But, contrary to what many do, that leads me to refrain from judging. I hesitate to rush to judgment about many things because, as Jews, we remained spared from one thing in all the unspeakable horror: from joining in. We had no choice, and he who has no choice—I mean, I had nothing against Hitler, it was he who had something against me—whoever has no choice has a limited capacity for judgment, cannot judge what fascinates others who stumble, who slide, who want, who are fascinated. For such a person it becomes a problem of fascination. It fascinates me to understand. And, given that I have gone to the effort of understanding existentially, as they would say in the dubious jargon of the history of philosophy, what this phenomenon of National Socialism is, what it is about, and in so doing got *absolutely* nothing from contemporary history or the historical sciences in general relevant to what *I* was interested in, I simply started with those who, on reflection, seemed right. As a young man (I've now gone gray), there already seemed to me no doubt that Martin Heidegger was during the 1930s the foremost exponent of philosophy in Germany; and there seemed to me no doubt that Carl Schmitt and Hans Kelsen were the most significant political theoreticians of the 1920s and the 1930s. And it seems to be completely surprising that both Carl Schmitt and Martin Heidegger entered into a liaison with National Socialism, a liaison for which no apology has any meaning. But it happened, and there was Freiburg National Socialism and there was the Schmittian variant; there is absolutely no doubt about that. The question is: what is it about National Socialism that can attract people like Heidegger and Schmitt? Now, of course, you can say that both are evil men, stupid men, or, of each of them, that Frau Heidegger got her husband into the Party, or you can suppose (and it has been said) that Schmitt is a boundless . . . he was that as well, of course, but does that explain a phenomenon of *violence?* What is going on there? There is something about National Socialism that I fail to understand, if I fail to understand how Schmitt and Heidegger felt any attraction to it. What did it mean to them, or, put another way, what have others forgotten, suppressed, displaced so this most terrible of all forms could see the light of day *and* attract people to it? Anyone who has taken a look at Ernst Bloch's *Erbschaft dieser Zeit* will have noticed an effort, an effort that others on the left have failed to make, to understand what was so fascinating in this, what kind of glittering dross this was. That was a line of thought that, very early on, made me not want to give up on Carl Schmitt.

To come to the point, for fascination itself is not enough. I have written about Schmitt for many years, and I am, in a manner of speaking, one of his obituarists (the *Frankfurter Allgemeine Zeitung* published a political obituary by Günter Maschke,[3] then Dolf Sternberger intervened as mentor and political teacher, made clear what democracy was, and so on).[4] We are always being told that Schmitt was no democrat, but that is not the point: no one had ever suggested he was. Schmitt had discovered something, or at least found something out: that democracy and Caesarism are not opposites. He was antiliberal, but democracy is not the opposite of Caesarism. The eminence, the esteem for democracy, that the majority thereby gain some kind of protection against Caesarism—we know from Karl Marx's *Eighteenth Brumaire* and from other situations and configurations that it is not so, and one should have known that later too.

Democracy and dictatorship are not in fact polar opposites. And Schmitt is in favor of dictatorship in the form of democracy. But let me come to the point. Herr Sontheimer, you are right: the two theses that I read in the article published in *Die Zeit:*[5] first of all the important thesis, if in need of some correction, that the left, if I might refer to it in this way, has a fascination with Schmitt, a particular section of the left. In fact the Frankfurt School followed a similar path in the Weimar period: Otto Kirchheimer was a student of Carl Schmitt, Hans Mayer as well. And in fact Habermas, Preuß, Claus Offe have picked up Schmittian topics, although I would say, from a closer acquaintance with Habermas, that he flinches from this for traumatic reasons. As regards the Suhrkamp "Theory" series, I have to defend Habermas here since he was always against the idea that we should involve Schmitt in Suhrkamp. It was Karl Markus Michel and Jacob Taubes who played with this idea. And it is to the honor of Schmitt that he said, "No, I don't want to have anything to do with Suhrkamp." Heidegger did the same, even though he was offered a large amount of money to publish *Sein und Zeit* as a Suhrkamp paperback,[6] a sum of money that was well beyond the going market rate. Both therefore had the backbone to say, "No, the Suhrkamp culture is not our culture." And I supported the idea, since in fact I believe that Schmitt is very important.

And with this we come to the point, that is, to politics. To the scary words *friend-enemy*. I have been in countless situations, in Habilitation presentations for political science or for other philosophical topics that have some connection with politics, where it was thought fitting to introduce some kind of criticism of Carl Schmitt, as if, when one talks of friends or of enemies, then one has always to talk of the friend-enemy couple. It is a form of analysis, and it is a question of whether this analysis concerns anything related to human existence. And I must acknowledge that the Maoist Schmittian, Joachim Schickel, has properly recognized that in his *Tageszeitung* obituary of 11 April 1985. We can recall the lines from *Concept of the Political:* "The distinction of friend from enemy denotes the utmost degree of intensity of a union or separation, of an association or dissociation. It can exist theoretically and practically, without having simultaneously to draw upon all those moral, aesthetic, economic or other distinctions. The political enemy need not be morally evil, or aesthetically ugly; he need not appear as an economic competitor. . . . But he is nevertheless, the other, the stranger."[7] The joke here as I understand it is that Schmitt was constantly concerned about the problem of hedging (*Hegung*). He says: there is war. Whoever condemns war as war, for example, the Kellogg-Briand pact, does not abolish war, not at all. Instead, he criminalizes war and thus makes it possible to prosecute war in the worst possible forms. Whoever opposes us here and now must be a criminal to be eliminated. That means that war becomes more acute, brutal, without any limits, if a state of war is not allowed to exist between men, a state of war that then brings about a peace. Whosoever denies this wants not peace but a more severe war. I don't think that this constitutes an apologia, since Schmitt had laid emphasis on this at several points in his writing, for instance, in *Ex Captivitate Salus,* which I recommend despite all reservations, since in it experiences are adumbrated that affect us all: "The enemy is our own question given form," that is, one can see oneself in it. He wrote this line for a few of us who visited him in a copy of the book. He thought that it was his task to note the reservations, concerns, and qualities of the enemy so as to limit hostility (*Feindschaft*).

It is now incumbent upon me to deal with what the chairman here has cited, and I will focus on the question of anti-Semitism. I must admit that when, as a student, I became interested in Schmitt, I was unaware of this dreadful 1936 meeting.[8] But it did not altogether throw me since I saw here the constitutive anti-Judaism of the Catholic Church. Erik Peterson, the great theologian, formulated it as follows: "The Church exists only on the assumption that the Jews, as God's chosen people, do not believe in the Lord." Only then and for that reason does the Church exist. Since I believe Carl Schmitt to be a profound Catholic thinker, and have good reason . . . [Interruption by Sontheimer: is Carl Schmitt an anti-Semite or not? Taubes responds: The Church is anti-Judaic, anti-Semitic] and I am now challenged to speak about this and I come to the second and difficult point. In the concrete constellation of declining belief since the later nineteenth century and early twentieth century, a "theozoology" took over from theology, and the racial element became important in this. I not only see that in Schmitt but also in Cardinal Faulhaber.[9] I can see it in other Catholic thinkers and dignitaries. I do not have to deal with this. I often asked Schmitt, and we can talk about this afterward, why he has not seen this or that point. I am happy to discuss this with you all. But I hope that in my initial presentation I express myself in such a way that you know what I consider important.

To take up your question, Mr. Chairman, of what is so fascinating about Carl Schmitt's critique of liberalism: I will reply with an anecdote. Herr Lämmert is the president of the Free University in Berlin, known to some of us here, he is an extremely courageous and liberal man of whom at one time I saw a great deal. I said to him, dear Lämmert, I really would like to be liberal; don't you think that I would like it? But the world is not so made that one can be liberal. For that is at the cost of others; the question is who pays the cost, and the third and fourth worlds, the fifth and sixth worlds that are approaching, they will not be liberal at all, but brutal demands will be made there. The question is, how does one deal with them, when one starts to deal with them? If you work only at this liberal level of democracy, you just don't see what happens in history. And now Herr Sontheimer asked me what fascinates me so much. Now it is hard to pull that all together, but I will try. In the "Corollaries" to the *Concept of the Political* there is an essay by Schmitt, a lecture that he gave during 1929 in Barcelona, "The Age of Neutralizations and Depoliticizations." Let me, if you permit, read the first few sentences of this. You will see what can fascinate me, Jacob Taubes.

We in Central Europe live "sous l'oeuil des Russes." For a century their psychological gaze has seen through our great words and institutions. Their vitality is strong enough to seize our knowledge and technology as weapons. Their prowess in rationalism and its opposite, as well as their potential for good and evil in orthodoxy, is overwhelming. They have realized the union of Socialism and Slavism, which already in 1848 Donoso Cortés said would be the decisive event of the next century.

This is our situation. We can no longer say anything worthwhile about culture and history without first becoming aware of our cultural and historical situation.[10]

Ladies and gentlemen, I believe that nothing has changed since then; in fact matters have only become more acute. "All signs point to the fact that in 1929 we in Europe still live in a period of exhaustion and efforts at restoration, as is common and understandable after great wars."[11] Nothing here has changed since the Second World War; we live in a period of depoliticized conventionality.[12] Kohl,[13] or whoever it was who was just here in Paris: his type represents this exactly. Perhaps it does not apply to the entire period following the First World War, but all the same: Carl Schmitt noticed how this era of restoration stood foursquare on very thin ice, but nobody else did. He was of the view that there was a major crisis coming. Following the Second World War, Europe reentered a period of cultural neutrality, a depoliticized "normality." Perhaps that was indeed necessary—even a time of healing, I have no objection to that. Intellectuals do not like to hear this, but, listen, the world is not arranged to please a few intellectuals, but so that people can live in it. Although I think that ultimately they will not live well. But I see that Schmitt's analysis, or at any rate his approach, can be of great interest. In terms of historical philosophy.

There is a second point that Herr Sontheimer has emphasized: decisionism. I will make just two points about this: the problem of decision and the problem that both Sontheimer and Berding have touched on, which I summarize in one word: *pure*. What does *pure* mean? Decision is what *Political Theology* is about, and that book starts with the line "Sovereign is he who decides on the exception." Now everyone asks: why a state of exception? But the exception is a fiction; it happens once in a lifetime; you can learn something from it if it happens just the once, but really once is nothing. I won't invoke Schmitt on this to start with, but rather someone who did address an issue similar to this, a Protestant writer with whom Schmitt ends his essay (he calls him a theologian, but he was not):

> A Protestant theologian who demonstrated the vital intensity possible in theological reflection in the nineteenth century stated: "The exception explains the general and itself. And if one wants to study the general correctly, one only needs to look around for a true exception. It reveals everything more clearly than does the general. Endless talk about the general becomes boring; there are exceptions. If they cannot be explained, then the general also cannot be explained. The difficulty is usually not noticed because the general is not thought about with passion but with a comfortable superficiality. The exception, on the other hand, thinks the general with intense passion."[14]

These lines were written by Søren Kierkegaard. He defined dialectical theology, dialectical philosophy whether in its Freiburg or its Frankfurt variant, variants which are much more similar than usually thought. Adorno started by working on Kierkegaard, if critically, while Lukács began with an important essay on Kierkegaard—if he had stuck with that both he and we would have been the better for it. I consider that, methodologically speaking, this represents a way into the problem, and Carl Schmitt took this route into political science in its broadest sense.

I will focus all that I want to say about Schmitt on this one word, the word *pure*. There is a kind of gigantism, a battle of the giants, in German thinking, according to which French thought is only a variant of German thought. I am not saying that, but others do. Years ago I taught here and tried to get the students to write about Bergson or Malebranche. But no, they wanted to work on Heidegger, without speaking a word of German, or they wanted to work on Nietzsche. I could not get anyone to write about something they could actually read. That gives you some idea. There is a similar gigantism that I associate with the word *pure*. It cannot have escaped your notice that the word *pure* plays a major role in philosophy; you only need to think of one of the most important titles in German philosophy, the *Critique of Pure Reason*. Which leads one to ask what that might mean, what is so pure, what does "impure" mean? How can reason be "pure"? What does "pure" mean, "pure" with regard to what, who has cleaned it? Well, those are funny questions, but I am thinking quite concretely. "Pure" means free of all experience, free from language, from history. That was already there in the dispute between Kant and Hamann. It might be that a few of you have already heard these names, although I don't mean Haman from the Book of Esther, but Johann Georg Hamann. Schmitt fought against one thing: a pure theory of law. A pure theory of law was a doctrine that took no account of actual history. Kelsen is more or less the main symbol here; the metaphor of purity is mixed with a strict positivism. I will present something from Kelsen and show that Kelsen would not be, or would not have been, capable of opposing the assaults of despotism. I cite from the *Allgemeine Staatslehre:*

> The claim that there is no legal order in despotism, but only arbitrary rule, is completely without meaning . . . even the state governed despotically represents some kind of order in human action. . . . This order is the legal order. To deny this the character of law is only a naivety born of natural law, or simple presumption. . . . What is treated as arbitrariness is simply the real possibility of the autocrat making all decisions himself, to determine unconditionally the activity of subordinate organs, and at any time abolish or revise once settled norms

with alternatives having either a general or special validity. Such a state
of affairs is a legal state of affairs, even if it is felt to be disadvantageous.
But it has some good aspects. The call for dictatorship in the modern
state based on the rule of law demonstrates this quite clearly.[15]

Kelsen wrote this in his *Allgemeine Staatslehre,* which was then translated into English as the *General Theory of Law and State.*[16] This passage is missing from the translation, although the theory has not
altered. It is, of course, missing because, as far as history is concerned,
the emergency finally arrived, despotism became visible, and Kelsen's
theory just collapsed. Schmitt understood that without the emergency first having to happen. When it did happen, he was then sucked
into it; there is absolutely no doubt of that. But he understood what
was at stake here: that whoever puts forward a *pure* theory of law is a
victim of absolute positivism, which means that any and every state
order must be obeyed.

※ ※ ※

I will now respond to three sets of questions: the problem of violence,
anti-Semitism, and Catholicism.

Regarding the problem of violence, I have only two stories to tell—
if "only" two, I nonetheless regard them as extremely important, they
represent a thorough confirmation of my point. After the Second
World War the rector of the University of Münster was Joachim Ritter, a philosopher who shaped an entire generation of philosophers, a
generation which today occupies the leading chairs of philosophy in
the Federal Republic—Odo Marquard, Lübbe, and so forth. Ritter
renewed contact with his former friend Eric Weil, who had been an
assistant of Cassirer; Weil lived in Vienna; Ritter sought conciliation
and offered him an honorary doctorate in Münster. It took a while
until it happened, but finally, in 1968, Weil agreed. An honorary doctorate means the following: you receive a document, and a lecture is

given on a topic of central interest to the person who is now an honorary doctor. Now Weil was a specialist in the problem of philosophy
and violence; his book *Logique de la philosophie* is probably—and,
unfortunately, a book forgotten in France today—one of the most
important philosophical texts to have been published here. He wrote
to the rector, who in the meantime was no longer Ritter but a chem-
ist, and it was 1968, and, you can imagine, he wanted to talk about
philosophy and violence. Ritter went to the rector and told him, and
the rector had a fit and shouted, Joachim Ritter told me, "Nothing
about violence, nothing about violence." Ritter thought, OK, he got
upset and he will calm down again. Or so he thought. The invitation
was printed: "We have the honor to invite you to the conferral of
an honorary degree on Dr. h. c. Eric Weil; he will present a lecture
on philosophy."

The second story. Schelsky had invited me, among others, to a conference; Gehlen was there and people of that type, someone called
Herr Wolff spoke, he was a jurist; he began his lecture on . . . In sum,
everything bad comes from the fact that we have not kept being pure
enough. I have never understood what that is supposed to mean. But
during the discussion I asked a question: Herr Wolff, I said (at the
time I did not know that this was the Wolff of the Marburg Manifesto,[17] a most reactionary academic, even before the student revolt), I
said, Herr Wolff, but there are problems, law does have a relationship
to the problem of violence and power. To which he responded, with
a certainty I found irritating: "Violence is not a part of my system."
Well, what can you say? That was my experience of the pure theory
of law.

Now to anti-Semitism. I have been asked whether I spoke with
Carl Schmitt about this. We *only* talked about this. Yes, he said,

> what do you want from me, are you an adherent of Peterson [Taubes:
> his foe, but also his friend], as I have quoted him: the Church only
> exists because the Jews have not accepted, because they do not live in

belief. The Church is consciously ambivalent, I am a Christian, there is no other way to be a Christian without a touch of anti-Semitism. But, and this is rather a hot potato, [Taubes: I jump forward a little] do you know, in the Gymnasium I had a choice of languages; I was not sure whether I would take Greek or Latin, and then French and English was possible, and then there was Hebrew. And then I chose Hebrew, the world language.[18]

In his head he had world Jewry and salvational history, which was a mixture of the latter and the history of peoples. We then came to a very difficult point, to his extremely unpleasant analysis of Friedrich Julius Stahl (I don't know if you know him). He was, of course, conservative to the bone, and Schmitt suspected that he was no conservative, but a Jew. I then talked about this with Gershom Scholem. And Schmitt was right; naturally that was an ambiguous existence, this F. J. Stahl. From our point of view, there is a problem. What about figures from the emancipation such as Heine? He signed his articles in the *Augsburger Zeitung* with the Star of David; that is not something that the printer added later. This is a secret sign from Heine that says: "I am neither French nor German, and I do not only belong to a Franco-German dialogue; instead I am Jewish. This complex—the entire emancipation—also seems to us a great deal more complicated; the balance of the emancipation is not unambiguous: to emancipate individual Jews, that they be permitted to vote, and so forth. What is of interest to us is what happens to our identity, and those on the liberal side, if you like, treat us badly. It was said, yes, as a person you are equal, but you must give up being a Jew. And so I say, as one who knows that a German is a German, a Jew is a Jew, and not simply a German of Mosaic confession: this is disgusting, unworthy nonsense the nineteenth century invented.

Now to Catholicism. Of course, the Church exists, a great and varied Church. I think Schmitt a profound Catholic thinker, as is Jacques Maritain, and the two are connected by the secret sign of Léon Bloy. Maritain did, as you know, belong to the Action française—I neither want nor can here rehearse the sins of the Action française—and there are similar kinds of developments in Schmitt. . . . I find it decisive that Schmitt understood history to be a way of thinking in intervals (*Fristendenken*), that time itself is a duration with a definite ending, and that has not before been made so clear in philosophical and theological reflection. I am no jurist, even if I know something of Smend and Heller; and it is also well known that a similar critique of liberalism comes from the Marxists. For me what is decisive is that I spoke with him, Schmitt, the first-rate theological and philosophical thinker.

The most important question is, in fact, that of morality, and there I dispute everything that Herr Sontheimer has said, by virtue of these principles: not only did he define the immorality of decisionism from a moral standpoint but he also forgot something fundamentally human: that a person, whatever that person does and says, does so in time. For example, we are involved in a dispute, and my chairman says that we have to end at some point. All things come to an end, at the latest on the Final Day. You just cannot go on discussing and discussing without end; at some point you have to act. That means the problem of time is a moral problem, and decisionism means saying the time available is not infinite. At some point in Parliament (not in parliamentary discussion)—it is all the same whether it is the prince with his privy counsellors or Parliament: their discussions occur in time, and at some point they have to act. And whoever denies this is amoral, simply does not understand the human situation, a situation that is finite and, because it is finite, has to make a separation, that is, has to decide. So I dispute that you judge from the point of view of morality, but think instead you judge from ignorance of the human situation.

Secondly, for Schmitt politics is not a domain. He is not a political scientist, a political theorist: he is a jurist. He could clearly have detached himself from any idea that he might be a political theorist for one very important reason: for Schmitt, politics is not a domain, but rather a degree of intensity, for everything can become political. A religious debate on the Trinity sounds theological, but if you are in Constantinople and you go on the streets to fight for the formula, then it is a political matter. Which means that "politics" is a domain that cannot be indexed from A to Z, but any human form can become political, when something becomes a matter of life or death or when an emergency looms on the horizon. So he is not a political theorist, but a historical philosopher, or a jurist, or rather both at the same time. Certainly, he is an occasional writer and thinker, a polemicist: God created systematic thinkers, and he also created occasionalists, and Schmitt only lights up when faced with a particular issue or problem. Schmitt is a concrete thinker, just the same way that Ernst Bloch is a concrete thinker. Simmel is here the forefather of all who have a feeling for a new philosophical style. I have been asked what it was about Schmitt that so fascinated me. Instead of giving my own answer, I will read out a letter that Walter Benjamin wrote to Schmitt on 9 December 1930, very late on in the Weimar Republic:

> Dear Professor,
>
> In the next few days you will receive my book *Ursprung des deutschen Trauerspiels* from the publisher. I write these lines not only to tell you this, but also to express my pleasure that I might, at the prompting of Albert Salomon, send it to you. You will quickly notice how much the book owes to your treatment of sovereignty in the seventeenth century. Perhaps I might go beyond that and say that I have also found in your later works, particularly *Die Diktatur*, a confirmation of my working methods as a philosopher of art deriving from your own approach to the philosophy of the state. If your reading of my book assists in your

understanding this feeling, then my intention in sending it to you is fulfilled.

Expressing my special esteem, your devoted

Walter Benjamin.

You can add my name to that.

1948–1978

THIRTY YEARS
OF REFUSAL

The history of Jacob Taubes and Carl Schmitt goes back to 1948; I will not recount it here, but tell you how it began. In 1948 I was a young upstart, I got a special grant from the Hebrew University, the Warburg Prize. I was in Jerusalem, that was after the division of the city, when the university library was in an enclave and out of bounds. I was ordered—professors were very much in charge, and if you want today to see an intact German university, then go to Jerusalem!—I was expected to study, or I was honored with the study of, seventeenth-century philosophy: Descartes (all Greek to me), Descartes to Spinoza. So I thought to myself: how can I get a handle on Descartes? I would like to understand what *loi*, *Gesetz*, law means. Is that a legal concept, is it a concept of nature? I was unclear about the nature of law in Descartes, and I remembered from my time as a student—then there was no theological dictionary where everything could be looked up—that there was a section on *nomos* in Schmitt's *Verfassungslehre*.

I went to the library and completed my book request for Schmitt's book—for express delivery since I had a paper to give. Well, the librarian looked at me with a mixture of pleasure and sadism—ha, it will be three months before a request like this will be ready. Three months? In three months the semester will be over, that is no use to me. I go to the head librarian, and get the same answer. More politely, and in a more friendly manner, he explains how things are: soldiers drive into the enclave, fetch books, put them in their trousers, bring them back, and so on. So no luck there. I cannot conjure anything up, and I am resigned. Three weeks later—not even three weeks—I got a call from the head librarian: "Come and fetch your book; it has arrived!" I did not ask why or wherefore. I was just pleased that the book was there. So I went to the library, and, so that I might not imagine that he had got the book especially for me, the head librarian told me what had happened. One day, shortly after I had put in my express request, there had been a call from the Ministry of Justice; Pinchas Rosen (earlier Fritz Rosenblut) needed the *Verfassungslehre* to work on the Israeli constitution (which, even today, does not exist, and will not exist, since the Orthodox Jews and the secularized Jews cannot find common ground). I was over the moon. Rosen had just sent it back to the library, "Now you can have it." I was thankful.

And then the following happened. Innocent that I am, I wrote a letter at the time to Armin Mohler, a not unknown personage, who had been a fellow student of mine in Zurich. You could say that he was on the extreme right and I was on the extreme left. *Les extrêmes se touchent*—at any rate, we had the same views about the middle. I wrote to him as follows. First of all, I told him the story. That happened. And I wrote: I just don't understand it—the fact that the two most important and intelligent men: the philosopher Martin Heidegger and the constitutional jurist Carl Schmitt, that they both flirted with the Nazis, however long it lasted. There is something there that I just can't understand; there is something about Nazism I just don't grasp, that it had such a fascination at all. Armin Mohler was at the time Ernst Jünger's secretary. And Carl Schmitt visited Jünger, and Jünger told him about the letter, and Schmitt got the letter, and he was certainly no slouch when it concerned propaganda about himself: he made copies of the letter. "Letter of a Jewish intellectual who understands more about me than all the rest," and so on.

I had no idea. Then my fate took me to America. It was a decision, and I had to find a job. And there—I assume it is much the same here—you have to do the rounds. You can either be brutal, or polite, depending on how one has been invited. I was invited to present a paper to a seminar run by a political scientist, Professor Eliot, whose sole contribution to science is that he introduced the word *organological*. (Which means that what we know from Othmar Spann he discovered in America.) Apart from that, I don't know what to say about him; I expect that he had a sharp assistant professor who really did all the work associated with the chair, and he was called Kissinger.[1] And it was he who invited me, not Eliot. He had heard that there was someone doing the rounds, so this person should come and give a paper. And I gave a paper on political theology, on Carl Schmitt, about his mystic phase, the democratic phase that Schmitt had, which presents a purely hierarchical cataract in *Political Theology I*. There is some sort of Heidelberg flair to this story. A young man came up to me and said, "Oh, I am so pleased to meet a friend of Carl Schmitt!" Me? Friend of Carl Schmitt? Never seen him and don't even want to meet him." "But I know your letter to Carl Schmitt!" Me? A letter to Schmitt? Never wrote one, don't even know where he lives. "But I have read it!" What was in it then? It was this same letter I had written to Armin Mohler, which he gave to Jünger, and which Jünger gave to Schmitt. The young man was Hans-Joachim Arndt, later professor of political science in Heidelberg, at that time a Humboldt student at Harvard.[2]

So I had been "spotted," as one says in these circles, and since then I received all of Schmitt's writings complete with dedications, references; he was very exact with that; he sent the books with pedagogical notes: "You must read that" and so forth. I never replied. The correspondence was one-sided. Then my fate drew me, if I can say such a thing, to Berlin—at the time I never dreamed that I would ever see Berlin. People urged me: "Go on, write him a card!" And I answered, "Carl Schmitt does understand what friend-enemy is, he knows that, for him, as a Jew I am an enemy *ex officio*, how can you ask me to send him a card? Everything is fine: he sends me his stuff with dedications, and I do not answer. He is sure that I have read it."

In 1967 I invited Alexandre Kojève, the interpreter of Hegel and to my mind the most important philosopher of that generation. I know that the universities do not share my judgment, but for me that is about as interesting as last year's snow. The people with whom I think or speak about Hegel know who Kojève is. And he came to Berlin, straight from Beijing—how he did that I don't know—and I had to look after him, which I liked doing, and I asked him, "Shall I book your ticket for when you leave? Where are you going?" And he said to me in his usual gruff way, "I am going to Plettenberg." He said: "Who else is there in Germany to talk to?" Hmmm, I thought, let's think about it. For twenty years people have said I should go and visit, and Alexandre Kojève, whom I regard as the most important philosopher, is going there. It may be a quirk of mine, I admit, but I stood firm: I didn't go.

Then Hans Blumenberg wrote to me: "Put a stop once and for all to this 'how did he say that'?—as if everything were a tribunal—you, Kojève, and Schmitt, you are all the same, what's the point?" It was an unusually friendly and intense letter from Blumenberg, for me I mean; others still get friendly letters today. So I said to myself: Listen, Jacob, you are not the judge, as a Jew especially you are not the judge, for you must admit that if you have learned anything, then you have learned it from Schmitt. I know about the Nazi period. I know a lot more, one part I cover with priestly silence, withheld from the public. You are not the judge, because as a Jew you were not party to the temptation. In a sense we were blessed, that we could not be party to that. Not because we did not want to, but because we were not allowed. You gathered here can make judgments, since you know about the resistance, for my own part I cannot be certain of myself, I cannot be certain that anyone would fail to succumb to the national uprising, and for one or two years go mad, unbridled, as he was. A great deal can be said about the lack of restraint in Carl Schmitt.

※ ※ ※

So I knew all that, almost all. He himself then showed me documents that made my hair stand on end—documents that he still defended. I really cannot bear to think about it. In any case, the Schmitt that I met was the post-*Politische Theologie II* Schmitt, that means thirty-five years after *Politische Theologie I*, after Peterson's attack. His final work in old age went back to this critique by Peterson, a critique that was monstrously effective. We never talked about a cult. We were distanced, but it was not without meaning for me to have spoken with a public jurist (*Staatsrechtler*) about violence, and he got me to explain, quite spontaneously, unsought for, undidactically, the background to Romans 9–11. And he said to me: "Before you die, tell some people about that." Today, seeing it clearly before me, that is an enormous statement.

Liberalism did not die at the hands of Schmitt; the left also developed a critique of parliamentarianism, the radical left. He was the anti-Bolshevik. If I understand his work at all, then he is the only person to have realized what is going on, that a global civil war is happening. Even after the Second World War. He could have been a Leninist, but he was made for the anti-Leninists. That it all disappeared into the Hitlerist swamp is the most fatal, but not the only, consequence. That would be to write the history of the Weimar Republic from the standpoint of how it ended. That history would be teleological in nature. This is one possibility—and the worst. But it is not my job to teach German history, or even to defend it, but to say that German history is all a preamble to Hitler, whether from Luther, from Bismarck, from Charlemagne, from Schmitt—I don't believe that. These genealogies are cheap, they cost nothing and can be easily set up. If it had happened in France, I could have presented you with Maurras to Gobineau. There is no skill in this, genealogies cost nothing, just time in a library. It did not happen that way, those were open possibilities that were then closed off.

We are not here talking about Schmitt's character. It is not my place to make judgments on someone who made peace with the Church, died as a member of the Church, and was buried by the bishop of Limburg—who am I to pass judgment? But I can only say to you, if we are now talking of political matters, that Schmitt made a warning in 1932. He wanted to exclude the communists and the Nazis and establish presidential government for four years, hold fast to Paragraph 48 of the Weimar Constitution until these radical forces undermining the republic disappeared or, at least, became insignificant. Let me tell you, if I had to choose between democracy and a government seeking to obstruct the Nazis using Paragraph 48, I would have no doubt which I would choose.

And now to the final point: even I do not understand it, but I will tell you about it. It is one thing to be a theologian, another to be a philosopher, and yet another to be a jurist. In my experience, these are quite different ways of understanding the world. The jurist has to legitimize the world as he finds it. This is rooted in his training, in the entire conception of the position of being a jurist. He is a man of intellectual integrity; his task is not to make law, but to interpret it. Schmitt had one interest: that the Party, that chaos did not win out, that the state stood firm. At whatever cost. For theologians and philosophers that is difficult to appreciate; but for lawyers, so long as a legal form can be found, whatever hairs have to be split, it simply has to be done, otherwise chaos rules. That is what he later called the kathechon: the restrainer who holds back the chaos bubbling up from the depths. That is not the way I think about the world, that is not my experience. I can see myself as an apocalyptic: it can all go to hell. I have no spiritual investment in the world as it is.[3] But I understand that another does invest in this world and sees the apocalypse, in whatever shape or form, as the adversary and does everything to subjugate and suppress it, because, from there, forces may be released that we are incapable of mastering. You see what I want from Schmitt—to show him that the division of powers between the terrestrial and the spiritual orders is *absolutely necessary*; if this demarcation is not made, then we are lost. It was this that I wanted to put to him against his totalitarian orientation.

I have thought about the problem for a very long time and found something in common between Carl Schmitt, Heidegger, and Hitler—well, you can take that *cum grano salis*, but it is meant quite seriously. Can you think what? I'll put it to you as a puzzle then. There is something very deep that they share in common. What does Adolf Hitler as a person, Heidegger as a person, and Schmitt as a person share in common? I will tell you what I think without any further ado. I will be very concrete. My first thesis is: German culture during the Weimar Republic and also the Wilhelminian era was Protestant, with a slight admixture of Jewishness. That is a *factum brutum*. The universities were Protestant. Of course, there were Catholic enclaves, there somewhere in Munich a kind of contra-university, and then perhaps Bonn and so forth, but that did not count, not at all in exegisis. *Catholica non sunt legenda.*

My second thesis is: all three are lapsed Catholics. That is no small matter. And now to the two intellectuals: they did not feel comfortable and secure in the German university, so they seized their place in a gesture that destroys all that came before, the Protestant-Jewish consensus, a consensus for which the name Ernst Cassirer is a sweet-smelling and elegant representative. These are people driven by resentment, that is the first point, but who, with the genius of the resentful, reread the sources. Heidegger, the pupil of the Jesuits, did such a work of rereading. He read Calvin, he read Luther, he read Kierkegaard. For us—I mean us, you and me—that was part of our education; we got that as part of our education. Karl Barth's *Römerbrief* caused a bit of a fuss,[4] but in principle these were things that were part and parcel of cultural Protestantism. There was a bit of a frisson, that was no longer the old Troeltsch—thinking of the 1920s—the old liberal synthesis, instead there was something going on!

But even that was admitted, you could discuss it over tea, because that was all part of how you were. But for Heidegger—that was all new to him. And he read it with quite different eyes, with Aristotelian eyes. And something quite fantastic came of it, whether rightly or wrongly, but, at any rate, he read it differently. And this cultural Protestantism with a shot of Jewishness—at root however a faithless, chic intelligentsia, professors of philosophy—unsealed his lips.

I can only tell you the following: the Jew Emmanuel Levinas, who is now all over the media as a guru and so forth, he told me the following. He was at the time part of a group of students of Heidegger who all went off to Davos when Heidegger met Cassirer. It was all rather medieval. He, of course, came from Freiburg, was a phenomenologist, and so on. And the evening after the grand confrontation between Heidegger and Cassirer—when, by the way, Heidegger refused to shake Cassirer's hand—the students had a party. They restaged the debate, and Herr Emmanuel Levinas, who had very thick black hair, but that could be whitened with powder, appeared as Cassirer. His German was pretty poor, and so he walked over the platform saying two words only, repetitively: "Humboldt Culture." And there was a racket that even reminded one of Göring ("when I hear the word *culture* I get my revolver ready"). That was Emmanuel Levinas. And that is the atmosphere of 1931—that was what it was like.

The same with Schmitt. He was no Jew, but a legitimate Catholic anti-Semite—he had taught me all about Catholic popular anti-Semitism. At the time we both thought very little of Vatican II, which was supposed to bring about a mental change, of course. He was a climber from the despised Catholic minority. He was no Radbruch the Upstanding, whose chair was here in Heidelberg where he taught legal philosophy, he was no neo-Kantian. He was from a Catholic background, and that was that. You only need to read the first chapter of *Political Theology*. The first sentence is the most lapidary: "Sovereign is he who decides on the exception." But that is right! And then there is the quotation from Kierkegaard, which is quite overpowering. Liberalism had said: that is where public law (*Staatsrecht*) ends. But that is just where the problem begins! In a global civil war. Anschütz, quite certainly an important jurist, said, and Kelsen wrote in his *Allgemeine Staatslehre*: there is no lawlessness, even the worst dictatorship is rule governed (this astonishing statement is missing from the English edition). Here was someone who posed substantive questions, just like Heidegger. That was the fascination.

But this all leads me into areas in which I do have thoughts, but in an area for which I can claim no competence, although I consider those who claim such competence to be merely ignorant. That is something else. Most of the books about it are unbearable and have not the slightest sense of real forces and crises. There you can hear them running through their democratic ABCs, and the inaugural lecture of every teacher in political science has naturally to give Carl Schmitt a kicking, saying that friend-enemy is not the proper categorization. An entire science has set itself up to suppress the problem. If you think about it—this is just a joke compared to the set of problems that derailed Schmitt, but that were problems all the same.

Dixi, and I have not saved my soul, but I have told you how it has happened.

EDITORIAL NOTE

PETER GENTE

It was in 1961 that Jacob Taubes first came as a visiting professor to the Free University in Berlin, and in 1965 he settled among the Judaists in the Institute for Hermeneutics. I unpacked his library from the big crates in which they had been shipped from New York and was not a little surprised to find that almost every book by Carl Schmitt carried a personal dedication from the author. Soon Benjamin's letter was making the rounds of the institute, for which the reader of *Hamlet oder Hekuba* had been waiting, but that was missing from the edition of Benjamin's letters published by Suhrkamp in 1966.[1] Whoever is interested in Benjamin eventually comes across Schmitt and vice versa (cf. Rüdiger Altmann).

But at the time I did not dare to ask Taubes about his personal relationship with Schmitt. It was only the latter's obituary that resolved the puzzle. It was for this reason that we were so keen to put this book together. We met Taubes in the Exil restaurant in Kreuzberg; he agreed immediately (we had wanted to do a book together for a long time). Because of the 1952 letter, we wrote to Armin Mohler, who turned out to be very helpful, got from Taubes a photocopy of his 1979 letter, went to Paris to record the debate, showed him the transcript, talked a great deal about it all, and a few days before his death talked about the title. The last words we heard from him were: "Call it: with Carl Schmitt in loving argument, or something like that; that is in Heraclitus, you will have to look it up." We found the passage: παλίντροποσ ἁρμονίη—you do not understand, how something that divides joins to itself: harmony of opposites, or diverging harmony, like that of an arc or a lyre.

SOURCES

"Carl Schmitt. Apocalyptic Prophet of the Counterrevolution" was a lecture at the Institute of Philosophy, Free University, West Berlin, first published in the *Tageszeitung*, 20 July 1985.

The "Letter to Armin Mohler" and the "Passages from Letters of Carl Schmitt to Armin Mohler" were put at our disposal by their owner, Armin Mohler.

The "Letter to Carl Schmitt" was put at our disposal by Jacob Taubes.

We thank Brunhilde Wehinger and Werner Fischer, who helped in the transcription of the debate in Maison Heinrich Heine.

For the transcription from Taubes's last lectures in Heidelberg, we are very grateful to Aleida Assmann and Jan Assmann.

NOTES

INTRODUCTION

1. Herbert Kopp-Oberstebrink, "Between Terror and Play: The Intellectual Encounter of Hans Blumenberg and Jacob Taubes," *Telos* 158 (Spring 2012): 127.

2. Aleida Assman, Jan Assman, and Wolf-Daniel Hartwich, " Introduction to the German Edition," in Jacob Taubes, *From Cult to Culture: Fragments Toward a Critique of Historical Reason,* ed. Charlotte Elisheva Fonrobert and Amir Engel (Stanford: Stanford University Press, 2010), p. xix.

3. Jacob Taubes, *The Political Theology of Paul,* ed. Aleida Assmann and Jan Assmann, in conjunction with Horst Folkers, Wolf-Daniel Hartwich, and Christoph Schulte, trans. Dana Hollander (Stanford: Stanford University Press, 2004), p. 69.

4. Gianni Vattimo, *Beyond Interpretation: The Meaning of Hermeneutics for Philosophy* (Cambridge: Polity, 1997), p. 6.

     Nietzsche, aphorism 22 in *Beyond Good and Evil* (1886).

5. Gianni Vattimo, *After Christianity* (New York: Columbia University Press, 2002), p. 15.

6. Ibid., p. 13.

7. Giorgio Agamben, *The Time That Remains: A Commentary on the Letter to the Romans* trans. Patricia Daly (Stanford: Stanford University Press, 2005), p. 139.

8. Slavoj Žižek, *The Puppet and the Dwarf: The Perverse Core of Christianity* (Cambridge: MIT Press, 2003), series foreword.

9. Walter Benjamin, "What Is Epic Theatre?" (1968:151), quoted in Agamben, *The Time That Remains,* p. 139.

10. All in-text references in the introduction refer to the page within *Ad Carl Schmitt.*

11. For the full poem in translation see *Telos* 72 (Summer1987): 130, special issue, *Carl Schmitt: Enemy or Foe?*

12. Carl Schmitt, *Political Theology: Four Chapters on the Concept of Sovereignty,* trans. and with an introduction by George Schwab, with a new foreword by Tracy B. Strong, (Chicago: University of Chicago Press, 2005), p. 36.

13. Ibid: "The exception in jurisprudence is analogous to the miracle in theology."

14. The use of Schmitt the Nazi jurist in a post-Shoah word is subject of a wide-ranging argument amongst scholars, an argument that has expanded to include Heidegger via the philosopher's central identification with the Nazi state and philosophy. The use of Schmitt and Heidegger by left scholars raises complex issues concerning antiliberalism (left and right) and totalitarianism, antimodernism and totalitarianism, and the degree to which scholars may wish to separate ideas in text from ideas in concrete application. Do scholars of the left read and use Schmitt and Heidegger as insider warnings of what may yet occur, or is the left actually increasingly antiliberal, containing within it an often unacknowledged fascist potential? This note and introductory essay is insufficient—and indeed not the place—to discuss these issues in the detail necessary.

    For an introduction to the issues see the following: *Telos* 72 (Summer 1987): 109, 132, 142, 147; Emmanuel Faye, *Heidegger: The Introduction of Nazism Into Philosophy,* trans. Michael B. Smith, foreword by Tom Rockmore (New Haven: Yale University Press, 2009); Mark Lilla, *The Reckless Mind: Intellectuals in Politics* (New York: New York Review Books, 2001); Jürgen Habermas, *The New Conservatism: Cultural Criticism and the Historian's Debate,* ed. and trans. Shierry Weber Nicholsen, introduction by Richard Wolin (Cambridge: Polity, 1989); Stephen Holmes, *The Anatomy of Antiliberalism* (Cambridge: Harvard University Press, 1993).

15. Daniel Bell states that Taubes taught Torah to him, Irving Kristol, Nathan Glazer, Milton Himmelfarb, Arthur Cohen, and their wives. See Joseph Dorman, *Arguing the World: The New York Intellectuals in Their Own Words* (Chicago: University of Chicago Press, 2001), p. 108; see also Nathan Glazer, "Commentary: The Early Years," in Murray Friedman, ed., *"Commentary" in American Life* (Philadelphia: Temple University Press, 2005). Glazer discusses being taught by Taubes, who suggested the group also read Jung: "We were perhaps lead astray by Taubes, who was something of a misleader" (49).

16. Jacques Derrida, *The Gift of Death,* trans. Gary E. Wiles (Chicago: Chicago University Press, 1995). For an introduction as to how Derrida's "gift" may be applied more widely see John D. Caputo and Michael J. Scanlon, eds., *God, the Gift, and the Postmodern* (Bloomington: Indiana University Press, 1999).

17. Griel Marcus, *Double Trouble: Bill Cinton and Elvis Presley in a Land of No Alternatives* (New York: Henry Holt, 2000).

18. It must here also be noted that, as well as Schmitt and Heidegger, Benjamin, amongst others (Arendt, Jaspers, Kojève, Foucault, and Derrida), is castigated for supporting tyranny of either the left or the right by Mark Lilla in *The Reckless Mind.*

19. From Croce's essay "Why We Cannot Not Call Ourselves Christians" (1944).

20. Thomas J. J. Altizer, letter, 9 January 2012 (property of author).

21. Carl Raschke, "Preface," in Charles E. Winquist, *The Surface of the Deep* (Aurora, CO: Davies, 2003), p. xiii.

22. Ibid., p. xv.

23. Winquist, *The Surface of the Deep,* p. 182.

24. Gabriel Vahanian, *Tillich and the New Religious Paradigm* (Aurora, CO: Davies, 2005), p. 21.

25. Gianni Vattimo, with Piergiorgio Paterlini, *Not Being God. A Collaborative Autobiography,* trans: William McCuaig (New York: Columbia University Press, 2009), p. 168.

26. Gianni Vattimo, in Richard Rorty and Gianni Vattimo, *The Future of Religion,* ed. Santiago Zabala (New York: Columbia University Press, 2005), p. 54.

27. Malcolm Bradbury, *Stepping Westward* (London: Secker and Warburg, 1983 [1965]), p. 302.

28. Ibid., p. 312.

29. Jacob Taubes, "The Issue Between Judaism and Christianity: Facing Up to the Unresolvable Difference," in Taubes, *From Cult to Culture*, p. 45.

30. Ibid.

31. Ibid., p. 46.

32. Jacob Taubes, "Four Ages of Reason," in Taubes, *From Cult to Culture*, pp. 272–73. test

CARL SCHMITT: APOCALYPTIC PROPHET

1. Carl Schmitt, "Die deutsche Rechtswissenschaft im Kampf gegen den jüdischen Geist," *Deutsche Juristen-Zeitung*, no. 41 (15 October 1936): 1193–99.

2. Karl Löwith, *Von Hegel bis Nietzsche* (Zurich: Europa, 1941).

3. Carl Schmitt, "Sociology of the Concept of Sovereignty and Political Theology," in Melchor Palyi, ed., *Hauptprobleme der Soziologie. Erinnerungsgabe für Max Weber*, 2 vols. (Munich: Duncker und Humblot, 1923).

4. Max Weber, "Appendix II: Prefatory Remarks" to *Collected Essays in the Sociology of Religion*," in Peter Baehr and Gordon C. Wells, eds., *The Protestant Ethic and the "Spirit" of Capitalism and Other Writings*, trans. Gordon C. Wells (London: Penguin, 2002), p. 356.

5. Weber, "Appendix II: Prefatory Remarks," p. 358.

6. Ibid., p. 357.

7. Carl Schmitt, *Ex Captivitate Salus. Erfahrungen der Zeit 1945/46* (Cologne: Greven, 1950).

8. Carl Schmitt, *Die geistesgeschichtliche Lage des heutigen Parlamentarismus* (1923), translated by Ellen Kennedy as *The Crisis of Parliamentary Democracy* (Cambridge: MIT Press, 1985). —TRANS.

9. Carl Schmitt, *Political Theology: Four Chapters on the Concept of Sovereignty*, trans. George Schwab (Cambridge: MIT Press, 1985), p. 36 [Trans. revised KT].

10. See Fyodor Dostoevsky, *The Brothers Karamazov*, trans. David McDuff (London: Penguin, 2003).

11. Schmitt, *Political Theology,* p. 5.

12. Ibid., p. 36.

13. *Frankfurter Allgemeine Zeitung,* 17 April 1985.

14. Albert Salomon, *The Tyranny of Progress: Reflections on the Origins of Sociology* (New York: Noonday, 1955).

15. Lyman Bryson and Louis Finkelstein, eds., *Science, Philosophy and Religion: Second Symposium* (New York, 1942).

    Salomon also reviewed Taubes's doctoral dissertation, "Abendländische Eschatologie, Beiträge zur Soziologie und Sozialphilosophie," under the title "Eschatological Thinking in Western Civilization: Reflection on a Book," *Social Research* 16 (1949): 90–98. —TRANS.

16. Taubes is mistaken here. The German original contains no publication details, but the reference here is to "Religion of Progess," later included in *Tyranny of Progress,* which was in fact published in *Social Research* 13 (1946): 441–62, hence after, and not before, the 1941 conference. The passage to which he alludes can be found here on p. 459. —TRANS.

17. In fact, the editors make clear that Mohler told the original publisher that he was Jünger's secretary until 1953 and that he gave Schmitt the original of the letter, not a copy. —TRANS.

18. Carl Schmitt, *The Nomos of the Earth in the International Law of the Jus Publicum Europaeum,* trans. Gary L. Ulmen (New York: Telos, 2003), pp. 59–60.

19. Günter Anders, *Endzeit und Zeitenende—Gedanken über die atomare Situation* (Munich: Beck, 1972).

20. Paul's Letter to the Romans 9:4–5.

21. A reference to Benjamin's essay, "Paris, Capital of the Nineteenth Century." —TRANS.

22. G. K. Chesterton, "Wanted, an Unpractical Man," in *What's Wrong with the World* (London: Cassel, 1912), pp. 10–11.

LETTER TO ARMIN MOHLER

1. In *Faust,* part 2, act 5, Mephistopheles acts as overseer to "Lemures," *Lemuren* in the original, shades of the restless dead in Roman mythology.

Johann Wolfgang von Goethe, *Faust*, part 2, trans. Philip Wayne (London: Penguin, 1959), pp. 267f. —TRANS.

2. Karl Löwith, "Les implications politiques de la philosophie de Heidegger," *Les Temps Modernes* 11/14 (November 1946): 340–60; see also the remarks in Karl Löwith, *Weltgeschichte und Heilsgeschehen,* vol. 2: *Sämtliche Schriften* (Stuttgart: Kohlhammer, 1983), pp. 614ff.

3. Adalbert Stifter (1805–1868), Austrian poet and moralist. —TRANS.

4. "A new commandment I give unto you, That ye love one another; as I have loved you, that ye also love one another." —TRANS.

5. Rudolf Karl Bultmann (1884–1976), German theologian; Emil Brunner (1889–1966), Swiss theologian. —TRANS.

LETTER TO CARL SCHMITT

1 Carl Schmitt, *Der Leviathan in der Staatslehre des Thomas Hobbes* (Hamburg: Hanseatische Verlagsanstalt, 1938), p. 131.

2 Alfred Schindler, ed., *Monotheismus als politisches Problem: Erik Peterson und die Kritik der politischen Theologie,* Studien der evangelischen Ethik, vol. 14 (Gütersloh: Mohn, 1978).

3 Carl Schmitt, *Politische Theologie II* (Berlin: Duncker and Humblot, 1978).

4 Erik Peterson, *Der Monotheismus als politisches Problem: Ein Beitrag zur Geschichte der politischen Theologie im Imperium Romanum* (Leipzig: Hegner, 1935).

5 The German churches are financed by a separate tax that was first introduced in the early nineteenth century, and article 137, para. 6 of the Weimar Constitution formalized this. —TRANS.

6 A reference to Spinoza in Schmitt, *Der Leviathan,* p. 86, note 1.

7 Carl Schmitt, "Die vollendete Reformation. Zu neuen Leviathan-Interpretation," *Der Staat* 4, no. 1 (1965)—reference to Hans Barion and F. Kempf.

8 Leo Strauss, *Natural Right and History* (Chicago: University of Chicago Press, 1953).

9 C. B. Macpherson, *The Political Theory of Possessive Individualism: Hobbes to Locke* (London: Oxford University Press, 1962).

10 This discussion did take place in 1984, a few months before Schmitt's death. Taubes made Romans, chapters 9–11 the subject of four lectures

delivered in Heidelberg shortly before his own death: *Die politische The-ologie des Paulus. Vorträge gehalten an den Forschungsstätte der evange-lischen Studenten in Heidelberg, 23.-27.Februar 1987,* 3d rev. ed. (Munich: Fink, 2003).

EXTRACT FROM A DISPUTE ABOUT CARL SCHMITT

19 March 1986 in Maison Heinrich Heine. Taubes shared the platform with Kurt Sontheimer in a discussion chaired by Helmut Berding. Here only Taubes's contributions are included.

1. *Deutsche Juristen-Zeitung,* 1 August 1934, reprinted in Carl Schmitt, *Positionen und Begriffe im Kampf mit Weimar-Genf-Versailles 1923–1939* (Hamburg: Hanseatische Verlags-Anstalt, 1940).
2. *Deutsche Juristen-Zeitung,* no. 41 (15 October 1936): 1193–99.
3. "Positionen inmitten des Hasses," *Frankfurter Allgemeine Zeitung,* 11 April 1986.
4. "Irrtümer Carl Schmitts," *Frankfurter Allgemeine Zeitung,* 1 July 1986.
5. Kurt Sontheimer, "Der Macht näher als dem Recht," *Die Zeit,* 19 April 1985.
6. As a *Taschenbuch,* hence in a small and cheap format. —TRANS.
7. Carl Schmitt, *The Concept of the Political,* trans. George Schwab (Chicago: University of Chicago Press, 2007), end of section 2.
8. See the following note. —TRANS.
9. Faulhaber (1869–1952), archbishop of Munich and Freising, 1917–1952. As a representative of the Catholic Church, he welcomed the Nazi seizure of power and in 1936 met Hitler and Hess at the *Berghof,* after which he declared that "without any doubt the Führer lives believing in God." —TRANS.
10. Schmitt, *The Concept of the Political,* p. 80 (trans. Matthius Konzett and John P. McCormick).
11. Ibid., p. 81.
12. "Wir leben in einer Biedermeierei." The Biedermeier era, generally iden-tified today with interior design and poetry, lay between the Congress of Vienna and the 1848 Revolutions. —TRANS.

13. Helmut Kohl, at the time chancellor of the Federal Republic of Germany. —TRANS.

14. Schmitt, *Political Theology*, p. 15.

15. Hans Kelsen, *Allgemeine Staatslehre* (Berlin: Springer, 1925), pp. 335ff.

16. Hans Kelsen, *General Theory of Law and State,* trans. Anders Wedberg (Cambridge: Harvard University Press, 1949). As Taubes goes on to remark, the passage is missing from the English translation, which is, however, not a direct translation of the *Allgemeine Staatslehre.* When Leo Strauss questioned the exclusion of this passage (*Natural Right and History* [Chicago: University of Chicago Press, 1953], p. 4), Kelsen argued that the omitted passage only related to a "particular application"; see "Foundations of Democracy," Kelsen, *Verteidigung der Demokratie* (Tübingen: Mohr, 2006), p. 364l, n. 13, reprinted from *Ethics* 66 (1955): 1–101. —TRANS.

17. The Marburg Manifesto was initiated in April 1968 by thirty-five Marburg academics opposed to recent proposals for the "democratization" of German universities, whereby students were to be given rights of participation in decision making. It was eventually supported by fifteen hundred signatories. —TRANS.

18. This passage is incompletely edited in the original. —TRANS.

1948–1978

This is the text of a lecture that Jacob Taubes gave on Paul's Letter to the Romans on 23 February 1987 in the Forschungsstätte der Evangelischen Studentengemeinschaft, Heidelberg. It has been transcribed from a recording that was made available by the Studentengemeinschaft.

1. Henry Kissinger gained his A.B. in 1950 and his A.M. in 1952 at Harvard, and so this has to be around 1953. —TRANS.

2. Taubes has earlier stated (p. 13) that Arndt was a Fulbright student, which is more likely; the Alexander von Humboldt Stiftung was only reestablished in 1953. —TRANS.

3. Sentence in English. —TRANS.

4. Karl Barth, *Der Römerbrief* (Bern: Bäschlin, 1919), translated as *The Epistle to the Romans* (London: Oxford University Press, 1933).

EDITORIAL NOTE

1. Carl Schmitt, *Hamlet oder Hekuba. Der Einbruch der Zeit in das Spiel* (Düsseldorf: Eugen Diederichs, 1956), p. 64.

Printed in the USA
CPSIA information can be obtained
at www.ICGtesting.com
JSHW021722300424
61830JS00010B/11/J